Success for Every Student

Success for Every Student

A Guide to Teaching and Learning

Second Edition

Shelly Pollnow and Oran Tkatchov

ROWMAN & LITTLEFIELD
Lanham • Boulder • New York • London

Published by Rowman & Littlefield
A wholly owned subsidiary of The Rowman & Littlefield Publishing Group, Inc.
4501 Forbes Boulevard, Suite 200, Lanham, Maryland 20706
www.rowman.com

Unit A, Whitacre Mews, 26-34 Stannary Street, London SE11 4AB

Copyright © 2017 by Shelly Pollnow and Oran Tkatchov

All rights reserved. No part of this book may be reproduced in any form or by any electronic or mechanical means, including information storage and retrieval systems, without written permission from the publisher, except by a reviewer who may quote passages in a review.

British Library Cataloguing in Publication Information Available

Library of Congress Cataloging-in-Publication Data Is Available
ISBN 978-1-4758-3562-5 (cloth: alk. paper)
ISBN 978-1-4758-3563-2 (pbk: alk. paper)
ISBN 978-1-4758-3564-9 (electronic)

Printed in the United States of America

Contents

Preface vii

Acknowledgments ix

Introduction xi

1   Setting the Stage for a Successful School Year 1

2   Classroom Management and Creating a Culture of Learning 5

3   What Are You Going to Teach Them? 15

4   High Expectations and Differentiation 27

5   Supporting School and Classroom Climate 35

6   Student Mobility and Attendance 43

7   Time on Task 49

8   A Deep Dive in Student Engagement 55

9   Multiple Intelligences and a Growth Mindset 65

10   Accessing Background Knowledge to Assist Learning 73

11   Reading Instruction for All Teachers 77

12   Writing Instruction for All Teachers 85

13   Assessing *for* Learning and Assessment *of* Learning: Did They Learn It, and What Evidence Do You Have? 91

14   Struggling Students: What Is an Intervention? 115

15	The Role of Coaching in Education	121
16	Professional Development for Teaching and Learning	127
17	How to Present Information to Peers	131
18	Some Parting Words from the Authors	135
Bibliography		139
About the Authors		157

Preface

With all the multi tiered interventions, assessment software, aligned textbooks, digital content, and scripted curriculum available to the field, some might question if the role of the teacher is significant in today's schools. Does it really matter who is leading the classroom? The answer to this question is a resounding YES!

Take a minute and think back to your favorite class. Chances are you do not remember the name of the textbook, the name of computer software, or the order in which the curriculum was taught. What you do remember is the person in charge of that class: the teacher.

For one of the authors, it was Mrs. Baron and her creative writing class. He does not remember what period it was or who sat behind him. He doesn't remember what literature was read or even the color of the textbook. He does remember Mrs. Baron making him feel like his work mattered and that he could do better. She showed genuine interest when he did a presentation on the punk-rock poet Henry Rollins and used that moment to convince him to write a paper comparing his anger to the rage in Maya Angelou's writing. Because of his teacher's encouragement, he had no problem learning about iambic pentameter or actually reading Maya Angelou during free time.

This interest was not instilled by a video collection, a laptop computer, or comfortable classroom furniture; it came from a teacher who possessed the skills necessary to get him excited to learn. The teacher-student bond and meaningful interactions are crucial to student engagement and academic success. Students must feel the support of their teachers while facing the challenges of learning.

Teachers face their own challenges as they grow and learn in the profession; many of them give up quickly because they do not feel supported or have the resources to hone their craft and feel successful. The purpose of this book is to help all teachers become confident in their teaching so that they can be the supportive force that students remember years later when they reflect on their school experience.

Acknowledgments

Many people have been instrumental in the motivation of this book. The authors would like to thank past and present coworkers, Mary (for all the help making this book worth reading!), Maddie, Alex, Luba, Luda, Tya, Kristen, Tony, Vinnie, and Lucie, and the rest of the Tkatchov/Korostil family, Dave Pollnow, Meagan, Mark, and Parker Pollnow/Murphy, John, and Mary Louise Kraynak and family, Geri and Jim Borgen, Anita Archer, Margaret Heritage, Tom Horne, Cheryl Lebo, Angela Denning, and Phyllis Schwartz.

Introduction

If I must start somewhere, right here and now is the best place imaginable.

—Richelle E. Goodrich

Like a blinking cursor on an empty page, it was just the first thing. The beginning of the beginning. But at least it was done.

—Sarah Dessen

Quality teaching is *the key* to student achievement. Although there are many new resources available to schools, research shows that the individual teacher's skills are still essential to student success. John Hattie compiled over 800 meta-analyses in his book, *Visible Learning,* and found that of all of the variables researchers study that impact the classroom, *teachers* have the greatest effect on and make the biggest difference in student achievement (Hattie, 2012). Other studies have resulted in the same conclusion: teacher quality appears to be more related to student success than class size and monetary spending (Darling-Hammond, 2000). Students of teachers who can convey higher- and lower-order thinking skills regularly outperform students whose teachers convey only lower-order thinking skills (Langer & Applebee, 1987; Wenglinsky, 2000).

In 2010, the *Los Angeles Times* published a story, "Who's Teaching L.A.'s Kids?" The *Times* used value-added analysis to look at the effectiveness of L.A. teachers based on student progress over a seven-year period (Felch, Song, & Smith, 2010). Their data showed the following:

- Effective teachers regularly took students who performed below grade level and boosted them to at or above grade level within one academic year.

- Many students (8,000) in the study had ineffective teachers for two or more years in a row.
- Effective and ineffective teachers were found in all schools, not just "rich" districts or "poor" districts. There was a wider gap in teacher effectiveness within a school than between the L.A. schools.
- A parent's choice of a teacher could be more influential in the student's success than the choice of school. Per the findings, a teacher could have three times as much influence on a student's academic progress as the school as a whole.
- A student's race, socio-economic background, previous achievement level, or English proficiency did not play a major role in whether or not a teacher was effective.

Prior studies (Sanders & Rivers, 1996) seem to confirm these newer findings that the teacher effect is "the most dominant factor affecting students' academic gain." How dominant of a factor? The same study showed that students who spend three straight years with the most effective teachers have a 50-percentile point advantage over students who spend three straight years with the least effective teacher.

Another study showed that in one school year, students taught by the top 5 percent of teachers were able to show 1.5 year's growth, while students taught by the lowest 5 percent of teachers showed only ½ a year's growth (Hanushek, 2009). Remember that it is common for a student to have an ineffective teacher for more than one year in a row. Based on these studies, the influence of a good teacher can alone mean more years of growth for an individual child. On the same note, the influence of a poor teacher can mean years of stagnation or falling behind grade-level peers. The most important resources in schools are teachers, and research shows that effective teachers using sound instructional practices increase student academic achievement.

At this point, one could argue, "Well, that's probably true for any profession. Those who get the better employees get better service." This is correct, but in the field of education, *all* teachers need to be effective because the final product is the future. A poorly made car, sofa, or meal can be easily returned or discarded. A poorly educated child cannot; factory recalls are not an option in education. There will never be a day when the evening newscaster announces, "Scottsdale High School issued a product recall on the graduating class of 2012. If you currently employ a member of the class of '12, please return him or her to the district office for a class of '17 upgrade."

High school dropouts are almost *four times* more likely to be arrested than high school graduates and more than *eight times* as likely to be incarcerated. Sixty-eight percent of prison inmates do not have a high school diploma

(Dropouts & Crime, 2008; Hanson & Stipek, 2014). Imagine what the world would be like if even half of these folks were able to finish high school.

As professionals working in a society where teachers tend to be the first to be blamed and the last to be paid, educators need to remind themselves that they have a higher calling as the instruments of change and as the voices necessary to elevate the profession. Devoting the time and energy to becoming truly effective teachers can bring about life-altering results for the children in their care.

Chapter 1

Setting the Stage for a Successful School Year

Exploring the old and deducing the new makes a teacher.

—Confucius

Ignorance is the curse of God; knowledge is the wing wherewith we fly to heaven.

—William Shakespeare

Quality teachers display a variety of personalities and appearances. Some are more traditional and formal, while others appear eccentric and over-the-top. Despite these differences, certain attributes of quality teachers remain consistent. Multiple sources suggest that exemplar teachers

- possess an adeptness to communicate to students,
- have a firm grasp of the content knowledge they teach,
- are lifelong learners,
- use different instructional approaches to meet the needs of diverse learners,
- are certified by the state in which they teach, and
- have experience teaching.

Other qualities of exemplar teachers include the following:

- *A continual focus on student learning.* Exemplar teachers know a good day is not based on whether their students listened quietly and stayed seated in neat rows, but what the students actually learned. The focus is on student learning, not the teacher.

- *A continual study of student work.* Exemplar teachers are always looking for evidence of what the students learned as well as what *exactly* they did not learn. These teachers are always looking at student work as a way to collect data and modify instruction.
- *Continual engagement of the students in the learning.* Exemplar teachers find ways to include problem solving and real-world applications into instructional practice. Real-world applications tend to keep students interested by answering the question, "Why do I need to know this?"
- *Continual study of the craft of teaching.* Exemplar teachers are up-to-date on best practices regarding classroom instruction, brain-based research, and current theory. Kids are always changing, technology is always changing, and therefore the teaching profession will always have to adapt.
- *Commitment to reflective practice.* Exemplar teachers always look back on a lesson to analyze what went right and how it can be duplicated. They also always look back on a lesson to analyze what went wrong and how it can be improved.
- *Goal-setting habits.* Exemplar teachers have a professional vision for growth, and they set reasonable yet rigorous goals for themselves and their classes.
- *Model good teaching.* Exemplar teachers model good teaching. It sounds silly, but most teachers *know* what good teaching is, yet their classroom practice does not resemble what they know. Knowing it is easy; doing it is the part that takes practice. Exemplar teachers bridge the knowing-doing gap.

It is no longer a guessing game as to what qualities are found in effective teachers or what needs to take place in a classroom to maximize learning and increase student success. Why doesn't it happen? Some teachers have had bad examples of what teaching should look like. Many teachers exhibit the teaching behaviors they saw when they were students or those behaviors imparted by their master teacher during their student teaching practicum. Some teachers replicate what they see other teachers doing in their school without knowing if what they are replicating is good practice. Some teachers are just burned out and buying time before they can retire.

Sometimes teachers fall into bad habits even though they have the best intentions. Once in the flow of teaching, some teachers tend to get comfortable even if they are not getting the wanted results. It's no different than trying to change a golf swing or eating habit. By no means is it easy, but with time, coaching, and consistency, the implementation of best practices and a handful of good instructional strategies will set the foundation for a successful and rewarding career in education.

Effective teachers need to have the commitment to model what is expected from the students and what is known to be effective teaching at all times. There are no shortcuts. *Teachers must commit to being committed.* They must wake up knowing they can and will do what is necessary to change a student's life for the better.

Now, the authors of this book are not fortune tellers, but they can predict what usually happens during the first year of teaching. How? Research, my dear Watson! In general, there are five phases that new teachers go through (Moir, 1999).

The first phase of a first-year teacher is the *anticipation phase*. During this phase, new teachers cannot wait to change the world and impart wisdom to a younger generation. Scenes from movies such as *Stand and Deliver* or *The Great Debaters* run through their minds. They are excited and feel incredibly prepared from their preservice classes to tackle the teaching job. The anticipation phase usually lasts for a few weeks.

The next phase is called the *survival phase*. Within a month, new teachers feel overwhelmed. Things are happening fast and situations occur that were never taught in college. It seems like there is never enough time to catch up on grading, and self-reflection is difficult because the new teachers are just trying not to break down or break something. Lesson plans seem to not work as expected, although a ton of time was used to create them. Amazingly, this challenging experience is what will help these teachers become better in the long term.

Following the survival phase is the *disillusionment phase*. After about two months of just surviving, new teachers tend to feel burned out or depressed, and some even question whether they chose the right profession. More work seems to be piled on as the first grading period ends and parent conferences begin. It has been noted that around this time many new teachers start to take sick days more often. Sounds horrible, right? Well, just when things seem like they couldn't get worse, they don't! After this phase, the frown turns itself upside down.

After being beaten down in the disillusionment phase, dedicated teachers find a way to pull themselves up by their britches. The fourth phase is called the *rejuvenation phase*. This usually begins around the winter break, when teachers get some well-deserved rest and relaxation. Teachers have time to reflect on what they went through and how they can do a better job when they return after the break. At this point, they put things into perspective. This phase will usually get the teacher through the rest of the school year.

The last phase is the *reflection phase*, which begins in the last couple of months of the school year. At this point, teachers look back at what worked and what didn't, and they begin thinking about how they can make the next year so much better. Teachers go through their first-year lesson plans and decide what to reuse and what to discard.

If you are a new teacher, hopefully the contents of this book will make your survival and disillusionment phases a little easier to handle so that you can rejuvenate, reflect, and work your way toward being an exemplar teacher, improving the lives of your students as you improve your practice.

REFLECTION SCENARIO

Think back and recall your favorite teacher. What qualities made him/her your favorite teacher? Which of the qualities mentioned in this chapter did that teacher exhibit and how? As a teacher, which of your own qualities do you want your students to remember when they reflect back on being in your classroom?

Chapter 2

Classroom Management and Creating a Culture of Learning

We cannot expect people to have respect for law and order until we teach respect to those we have entrusted to enforce those laws.

—Hunter S. Thompson

Manage others the way you would like to be managed.

—Brian Tracy

Classroom management is the underpinning of effective teaching. It is the foundation for student achievement, and it sets the stage for a culture of learning in which all feel safe to express ideas, make mistakes, and learn from mistakes. Teachers who cannot manage the classroom are not able to teach. *You will not survive as a teacher if you do not have effective classroom management procedures.* Most teachers who do not master classroom management leave the profession within the first five years of teaching.

According to researcher Robert Marzano, "A classroom that is chaotic as a result of poor management not only doesn't enhance achievement, it might even inhibit it"(Marzano & Pickering, 2003). Carolyn Evertson and Alene Harris noted that "teachers whose students demonstrated high on-task rates and academic achievement implemented a systematic approach toward classroom management at the beginning of the school year" (Evertson & Harris, 1992).The teacher, therefore, must set the stage to foster a culture of learning and allow for the deepest learning possible for all students.

RULES AND PROCEDURES

Consistent classroom procedures play a significant role in establishing a learning environment that fosters academic achievement and social growth. The adage "It is always easier to get nicer as the year goes on than to get tougher" holds some truth, but a more appropriate saying is, "Your expectations and consequences need to be consistent from day one until the final bell rings on the last day of the school year."

If a teacher lets a student do something on the first day of school, that teacher should expect him/her to continue doing it for the rest of the year. Good classroom habits and manners are not a result of happenstance; they are intentionally taught and reinforced throughout the year. It is important to give positive feedback for the actions one wants to see more often, and it is important to assign consequences and give feedback to correct the inappropriate actions that one wants to limit.

The first thing a teacher needs to do is create the "nonnegotiable" classroom rules and procedures and enforce them consistently—every day for every student. Rules are different from procedures, but both are needed to create an orderly classroom. *Rules* are meant to guide behavior, whereas *procedures* deal with the day-to-day processes in the classroom. A positive emotional classroom climate that fosters a culture of learning contains six aspects (Walker, 2004):

1. *Acceptance by the teacher.* The students need to know that the teacher believes they can succeed.
2. *Acceptance by peers.* The students need to know that they are part of a learning community and will not be hurt or put down. The sense of "belonging" to a school has many benefits, including reduced dropout rates, fewer discipline issues, and increased academic success (Christle, Jolivette, & Nelson, 2007).
3. *A sense of order.* The students need to know that the teacher has a plan and that there is a routine within the class.
4. *Clarity of tasks.* The students need to understand what they are expected to do.
5. *Resources for success.* The students need to know that they have access to the tools needed for success.
6. *Emotional intelligence.* The students need to know they can express emotion in the process of their learning.

For a safe and effective learning environment, teachers should have approximately seven rules for secondary classes and five to eight for elementary classes (Evertson, Emmer, & Worsham, 2003). Anything more than eight will be difficult for the students and teacher to remember. Although some rules are nonnegotiable, most rules are more effective when students have input and take ownership. By more effective, the authors mean there is a better chance the students will take ownership of the rules, obey the rules, and not question why the rules are in place.

As previously stated, procedures are the day-to-day processes in the classroom. These include how to turn in homework, how to enter and leave the classroom, how to get materials, and how to work in partners and teams. Author Harry Wong offers "The Three-Step Approach to Teaching Classroom Procedures" to be taught at the beginning of every year (Wong, 1991):

Explain: State, explain, and model the procedure. Students need to know why the rule is in place and the purpose behind it. Do not assume the student knows how to adhere to the rule. Model what "whisper" should sound like. Model what an organized desk looks like. Although this may seem like a waste of time, preventing any misunderstandings the first day will save the teacher time as the school year progresses.

Rehearse: Rehearse and practice the procedure under teacher supervision. Make sure the students are capable of performing the procedure. Sometimes the classroom layout will prevent a student from seeing the board or talking quietly to a partner. Students for whom English is a second language, for example, might have a different interpretation of the procedure. Through modeling and rehearsing, the teacher can ensure all students are "on the same page" and have a common understanding.

Reinforce: Reteach, rehearse, practice, and reinforce the classroom procedure until it becomes a student habit or routine. Repeat this process as needed. Remember the old saying, "If you expect it, then you must teach it." Reinforcing is the most important step, especially in the beginning of the year. Applaud students and give positive feedback for correctly following procedures (make them a positive example while providing positive reinforcement), and politely give corrective feedback to students who have yet to make them a routine.

Some students might test the teacher by diverting from classroom procedures. In these cases, politely and quietly remind the students of the procedures; compare their behavior to the rules and do not make it personal. Do not bring the attention of the class to the negative behavior. In time, the students will see that the teacher is not letting up and will adhere to the procedure. When these students demonstrate the correct procedures, quietly reinforce the positive behavior.

As the year progresses, consistently enforce the classroom procedures; periodically stop to state, explain, model, and demonstrate the procedure again.

This is important for all grades and age groups. Make sure that the classroom rules are posted in an area where they are observable to both the teacher and the students. To reiterate, *promote the positive examples and quietly correct the negative examples through specific and timely feedback.* Make it a standard routine to review, reinforce, and rehearse classroom procedures as new students join the classroom or after extended breaks and holidays.

No matter how much the teacher has to remind the class of the routines and rules, the teacher must enter the classroom every day with the mindset that students will follow the rules and procedures. Avoid beginning the day with the attitude that the class will once again be out of control. Keep expectations high and believe that all students will meet these expectations.

As stated earlier, rules are more effective when students have input and take ownership. There is a good chance that the students will want what the teacher wants for rules. The teacher can guide the conversation as students come up with suggestions to align with what the teacher wants to see in the classroom. For instance, in an elementary school, a student might say, "I don't want Jimmy touching my desk." The teacher can reply, "Okay, so we want to keep our hands to ourselves and respect one another's property? We can make that a rule. How many vote to make this a classroom rule?"

After creating the rules and the routines, the teacher needs to think about the consequences for not adhering to the rules and routines. Similar to "The Three-Step Approach to Teaching Classroom Procedures," involving students to some extent in the development of consequences for infractions often creates buy-in and serves to help students take ownership of the procedures, rules, and consequences. Develop a step-by-step set of actions that will occur if rules and procedures are not followed, explain and model the actions to the students, post the set of actions in the classroom, and provide a copy to parents. Note: The teacher will again want to guide the conversation as students tend to make consequences much more severe than necessary. This is especially typical in the younger grades.

The following is an example from a sixth-grade classroom as the teacher and students develop rules and consequences:

This was an inclusion class with 34 students, which included two students with severe cognitive disabilities, nine students qualified as gifted, seven students qualified for special education services, four students identified as English Language Development, a para professional, and a general education/gifted education teacher. Twelve of the students qualified for free and reduced lunch.

The school did not have a school-wide discipline program, but there were school rules in place. The class began the process of developing rules and consequences for their classroom on the first day of school. The teacher set the stage by reminding the class they would probably be living and spending as much time together in their classroom during the school year as they spend at home with their families.

Since it was quite likely that there would be times when all 36 people would be in the 20' × 18' space, rules and consequences would have to be in place to guide behavior and promote a safe and productive environment for their classroom. There were sheets of posters situated around the room. One poster listed the school rules with the consequences and other posters listed nonnegotiable classroom rules with consequences as well as blank posters for "Additional Rules and Consequences" as a heading. Students in teams rotated around the room discussing the rules, adding comments and any additional rules and consequences that they thought might be necessary. The teacher guided the classroom discussion on what rules and consequences would be appropriate to make their classroom a place of safety, productivity, and respect for both students and teachers.

Consequences should be in accordance with the school's student handbook and must *never* humiliate or disrespect the student. Once upon a time, there was a belief that embarrassing students who misbehaved would teach them a lesson and prevent them from breaking rules again. Publicly embarrassing students will *not* make them better students. What it will do is make them despise school and despise the teacher! It is not the severity of the consequence that will make a difference in the classroom, but the consistency in enforcing the rules.

When delivering a consequence, do not make it personal. The teacher must try to remain calm and unemotional, explain the inappropriate action, remind the student of the positive action he/she would like to see, and then get back into the mode of teaching. Do not make the delivery of the consequence a huge, theatrical event.

Most importantly, listen to the student's explanation for why the behavior occurred. Actions of effective listening include

- fully attending with mind, body, and heart;
- listening with the intention of understanding what the speaker is trying to communicate;
- setting aside whatever may interfere with focusing on the speaker and the message;
- paying attention to the total message, verbal and nonverbal;
- being empathetic to the feelings being expressed;
- refraining from judging the speaker, the communication style, or the message; and
- being patient (Fitterer et al., 2004).

Even though the child's action was inappropriate, it is important that the teacher hears from the student why the behavior happened and then provides timely and specific feedback, which includes a way to correct the behavior in the future. This cannot occur if the teacher does not listen to the student's explanation for the behavior.

PHYSICAL ARRANGEMENTS

Along with teaching and reinforcing rules and procedures, a successful teacher intentionally arranges classroom space to allow for an unimpeded, yet structured, flow of teaching and learning. The physical arrangement of the classroom is just as important as classroom procedures in creating a manageable classroom.

Harry Wong predicts that the very first thing an effective teacher will ask of a student is for the student to find his/her assigned seat. *Do not let students pick where they want to sit!* A classroom arrangement that is not beneficial to the student (e.g., a student with low vision is sitting where he/she can't see the board or a very social student is sitting next to another chatty friend) can affect student learning by as much as 50 percent (Black, 2007). The following are best practices for the physical arrangement of the classroom:

- Seating arrangements should support the purpose of the lesson format; therefore, it is important that the room configuration be flexible and changeable.
- Students who need more monitoring, the "high maintenance students," should be seated at the front of the class, or where the teacher can easily see them, as well as away from anything that can provide a distraction. Teachers also need to check individual education plans (IEPs) to accommodate students with disabilities.
- Students should rehearse and practice a limited number of room configurations that will support a few basic learning structures, just as students practice and rehearse procedures (Evertson & Harris, 1992).

Here are examples of different seating configurations:

Classroom-style seating (Figure 2.1) is the traditional setup. This arrangement is good for times when the teacher will conduct large-group direct instruction and for testing. The high-maintenance student is in bold (see Figures 2.1, 2.2, & 2.3).

Classroom Management and Creating a Culture of Learning   11

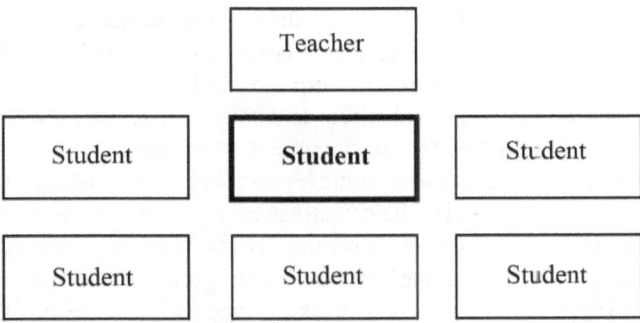

Figure 2.1   **Classroom-Style Seating.** Adapted from Wong & Wong (1991).

Pod-style seating (Figure 2.2) works well when students are working in teams or centers. This arrangement provides the students with a common work space.

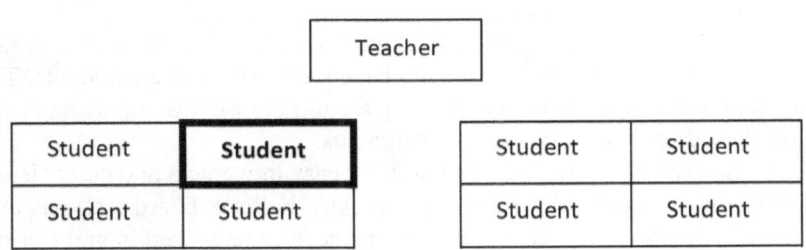

Figure 2.2   **Pod-Style Seating.** Adapted from Wong & Wong (1991).

U-shaped seating (Figure 2.3) works well when the students will be working with a partner as well as individually. This arrangement allows everyone the ability to listen to the teacher for direct instruction portions of the lesson.

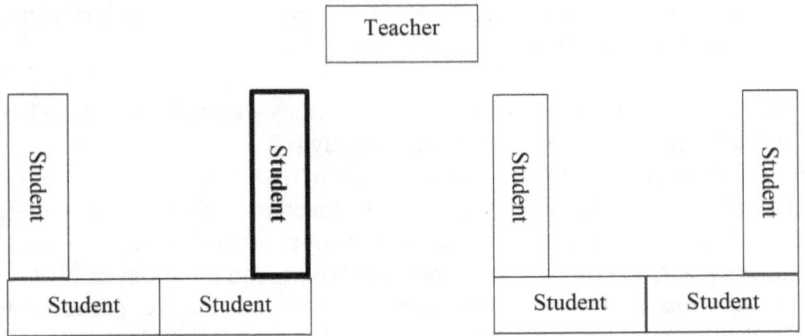

Figure 2.3   **U-Shaped Seating.** Adapted from Wong & Wong (1991).

The class seating chart should change throughout the semester, and the students should be aware that the seating chart will change often. In the beginning of the year, a seating chart will help the teacher remember the names of the students as well as assist substitute teachers. The seating chart should be written down and used as a tool to document attendance.

As personalities and student achievement become evident, the seating arrangement should maximize the effectiveness of the room. Partners for reading or math should be close to each other. Some teachers, especially in elementary grades, will change the classroom configuration throughout the day.

Research suggests using a good masking tape to mark the position of the desks for the most often used arrangement (Jones, 2000). This will help reduce time when returning to the standard arrangement. Check with the school janitor to see if this is okay for the floors (if he/she says no, then ask the principal and explain why this will be beneficial to the class). It is important to be able to change the arrangement of the class with as little effort or as few distractions as possible.

The physical arrangement of the classroom should allow the teacher to easily move throughout the classroom and have clear access to all students. The area where the teacher will be delivering the direct instruction portion of the lesson should be clearly visible to all students.

If the classroom design does not allow for easy movement and clear vision, then the classroom must be redesigned. Any bulletin boards, televisions, artifacts, computer screens, and other items need to be placed in areas of the room that do not block the teacher's vision of the classroom or block access of movement. Make sure all student materials (books, backpacks, etc.) are also placed in appropriate areas. These items should be placed where they cannot be a distraction to the students or where the teacher and students will not stumble over them.

The CHAMPS framework for classroom management helps teachers set up a classroom for success. CHAMPS is the acronym for the following framework that supports positive learning environments and behaviors (Sprick, Garrison, & Howard, 1998):

- *Conversation*—Are students seated where they can talk to each other if needed? What is the voice level for the activity?
- *Help*—What do you do when you need help?
- *Activity*—What is the activity you will be teaching them? Will it be engaging? Chapter 8 will address the important topic of student engagement.
- *Movement*—Can you and the students move around the room safely?
- *Participation*—How will you know if the students are participating? What does "participation" look like? Do the classroom rules support this behavior?

Even with all of these strategies and structures in place, some students will still have difficulties and behavior issues. For those students who continue to test the classroom rules, other approaches might be needed.

Researching the cause is necessary. One approach to addressing a difficult student's behavior is to ask other teachers, such as the teacher from last year, if they witnessed these behaviors and how they handled them. Rely on colleagues to assist in finding the cause of the behavior, and identify what other teachers have done to help the student. If other teachers did not experience the observed behavior, it is time to involve the parents and the student in a conversation to help to get the student back on track.

In some cases, it takes a team of people to identify the issue. For example, *sensory processing* (the way the nervous system receives and sends information from the senses) has recently been identified as something to assess in elementary children who exhibit behavior issues (Fox, Snow, & Holland, 2014). One study showed that at least one in every six children who struggle in the classroom suffer from a sensory processing disorder (Ben-Sasson, Carter, & Briggs-Gowan, 2009). In these cases, experts beyond a classroom teacher, such as an occupational therapist, need to be included in the discussions.

Another option may be to design a behavior plan. A *behavior plan* is a formal plan that addresses an individual student's behavior. Typically, the student, the parent(s), and all teachers of the student are involved. When writing a behavior plan, start by identifying the behavior that needs to be corrected or redirected. Make sure that the identified behavior is measurable, specific, and overt. Saying, "He gets on my nerves," is not measurable, specific, or overt.

It is important that the behavior is measurable so the teacher can provide data on when, how often, and for how long the behavior has occurred. Collect classroom data when the child tends to misbehave or when the outbursts tend to happen. Note what triggers the misbehavior. The key is to find out when the outbursts occur and why the student reacts that way so that the disruptive stimulus can be changed or the reaction to the stimulus altered.

Once the behavior is identified, the teacher, with input from the student and parents or guardians, decides what replacement behavior or intervention is to be put in place. Ask the student what tends to trigger the behavior and what events in the classroom make him/her respond inappropriately.

Once these items are noted, come up with alternative behaviors the student will exhibit, or replace the item that triggers the poor behavior if it is appropriate for the rest of the class. The teacher needs to explicitly provide the student with examples of what the replacement behavior looks like in specific situations. Provide concrete, tangible examples to make sure the student understands all rules, new behaviors or routines, and consequences (Lavay, French, & Henderson, 2007).

Lastly, keep track of the behavior plan to monitor whether or not it is working. Are the behaviors happening less often? Is the student exhibiting the replacement behavior more often? Is the teacher reinforcing the replacement behavior by acknowledging it? If at all possible, involve the student in collecting the data.

Rules, procedures, and a classroom setup to accommodate various learning formats will help teachers to maximize instructional time and foster a culture of learning throughout the school year. These structures allow the teacher to begin the actual art of teaching and create a safe learning environment in which the teacher and students function as a productive and respectful team.

REFLECTION SCENARIO

Mr. Raul, a first-year teacher at Frehley High School, has had the same instructional routine since he began teaching in August. It is now October, and as students enter the room, he tells them to sit wherever they wish. He then takes attendance as students talk to their friends; it takes him ten minutes since they are not in assigned seats, but he thinks the class will be more enjoyable if the students get to sit with their friends. As soon as Mr. Raul finishes recording attendance, he gathers his notes and begins lecturing for the next 45 minutes to his class of 30 students. The desks, which had been in six neat rows, are now askew. A few students take notes, but most continue talking.

Mr. Raul asks the students to "keep it down," and he raises his own voice as the lecture progresses to talk over the chatter in the classroom. With five minutes to go, and his voice just discernible above the din, Mr. Raul stops, asks if there are any questions, and assigns homework. Mr. Raul teaches next door to your room. After school, he comes to you in desperation, truthfully describes his class, and asks for your help. How do you respond?

Chapter 3

What Are You Going to Teach Them?

Through learning we re-create ourselves. Through learning we become able to do something we were never able to do.

—Peter Senge

If the education of our kids comes from radio, television, newspapers—if that's where they get most of their knowledge from, and not from the schools—then the powers that be are definitely in charge, because they own all those outlets.

—Maynard James Keenan

Effective classroom management is only one part of being a successful teacher. Content area knowledge (mathematics, English, social studies) is also important, but so is knowing exactly *what* is supposed to be taught to the students and *when* they are supposed to know it. This is called having a *guaranteed and viable curriculum*. A guaranteed and viable curriculum is a plan of what the teacher will teach and what the students will learn (Marzano & Pickering, 2003).

The curriculum is basically all the planned opportunities to learn that a student experiences under the direction of the school (Festus & Kurumeh, 2015). These opportunities to learn can be taught in the time provided; have explicit and specific objectives for every subject area, grade level, and course; and are based on an academic standard.

STANDARDS VERSUS CURRICULUM

It is important to note the difference between the terms "standard" and "curriculum." The two terms are fundamentally different and are often misused when discussing educational content and expectations of learning. The *standard* is the knowledge or skill that the student is expected to know at a certain grade level. The standard does *not* explain how a teacher should teach or what materials to use.

The Every Student Succeeds Act (ESSA), the federal law that governs U.S. public education policy, requires each state to have standards that align with college and career readiness. These standards are mandated by the state for public districts and public charter schools to meet. Some states have created their own academic standards, or in the case of the Common Core State Standards, some states have chosen to use a set of standards that are being shared across multiple states or regions.

Here is an example of an academic standard from the Grade 6 ELA Common Core Standards:

CCSS.ELA-Literacy.W.6.3

Write narratives to develop real or imagined experiences or events using effective technique, relevant descriptive details, and well-structured event sequences.

- Engage and orient the reader by establishing a context and introducing a narrator and/or characters; organize an event sequence that unfolds naturally and logically.
- Use narrative techniques, such as dialogue, pacing, and description, to develop experiences, events, and/or characters.
- Use a variety of transition words, phrases, and clauses to convey sequence and signal shifts from one time frame or setting to another.
- Use precise words and phrases, relevant descriptive details, and sensory language to convey experiences and events.
- Provide a conclusion that follows from the narrated experiences or events.

   Retrieved from: http://www.corestandards.org/ELA-Literacy/W/6/#CCSS.ELA-Literacy.W.6.4

Here is another example of an academic standard from the Grade 8 Mathematics Common Core Standards:

CCSS.Math.Content.8.NS.A.1

Know that numbers that are not rational are called irrational. Understand informally that every number has a decimal expansion; for rational numbers show that the decimal expansion repeats eventually, and convert a decimal expansion which repeats eventually into a rational number.

Retrieved from: http://www.corestandards.org/Math/Content/8/NS/

Before deciding what to teach, it is imperative that the teacher look at state academic standards and become comfortable with those standards for that grade level as well as the standards for that grade band. For example, a fourth-grade teacher will need to know the fourth-grade standards and also be aware of what the students were previously taught (third-grade standards) as well as what they will be expected to know in the next grade (fifth-grade standards).

The *curriculum* is the plan of what the teacher will teach and what content (from the standards) the students will learn. The guaranteed and viable curriculum basically pinpoints what content is critical for all students, sequences it in a way that makes sense, provides sufficient time for students to learn it, and ensures teachers attend to the content in the classroom. As mentioned earlier, the standard does *not* explain how a teacher should teach or what materials to use; this is the role of the curriculum. The curriculum includes the way the content will be taught and the materials that will be used to teach and assess that standard. A textbook, for instance, would be a tool used with the curriculum, but by itself would not be considered curriculum. Math manipulatives would be a tool used within the curriculum to teach the standard.

The standard—in collaboration with textbooks, educational materials, lesson plans, and other materials or directives—creates the curriculum. Standards tend to remain constant, while the curriculum can be periodically (or annually) changed at the school or district level or often at the classroom level to ensure students are meeting their academic goals (Chenoweth, 2014).

The sequence of the curriculum, or the order of content taught, should make sense. What is taught first should help the student understand what will be taught next. A successful curriculum sequence will be ordered so that previous knowledge helps the student learn new concepts. There should be a progression of skills and knowledge. This is what researcher Margaret Heritage (2010) refers to as *learning progressions*. Teachers well versed in their content areas understand the building blocks of a learning progression for an important concept to be taught and the proper sequence to ensure a student's depth of learning and their ability to transfer knowledge and skills in new situations.

Most successful schools already have a curriculum in place and expect teams of teachers to discuss the curriculum and monitor the standards quarterly or annually to ensure the curriculum is still guaranteed and viable. Many high-achieving schools have grade-level or department-level teams that meet on a weekly basis for planning and data discussions that include aligning lessons and pacing with their school's curriculum.

These successful schools have *curriculum maps*, also called pacing guides, to help the teacher map out the content for the semester or school year. Per experts in this field, a curriculum map is the product of "the process where each teacher records the content that is actually taught, how long it is taught and how they are assessed and aligned to academic standards"(Udelhofen, 2005). It is important that the teacher follow grade-level content and be provided district or school curriculum maps to assist in mapping out the content for the day, week, month, and semester.

Depending on the school or district, some curriculum maps are created at the school level by teachers during the summer or school year, while some maps are created at the district level. Either way, it is the expectation that the teacher follows the curriculum map while still having a little flexibility based on the needs of the specific class. For example, if a student who is deaf or hard of hearing is in the class, the teacher will need to take that student's language and communication needs into consideration and guarantee every student's access to the content or assessments within the curriculum map. If a teacher is struggling to teach the content within the time provided on the curriculum map, it is crucial for the teacher to talk to his/her colleagues or academic coach about modifying the timeline of the map or get some guidance on how to teach within the map's limits.

Figure 3.1 is an example of a curriculum map from LaRue County, Kentucky.

The map is separated into specific parts: a timeline, the content, the concepts, the processes, and the assessments. Maps will vary depending on the school or district, but all functional maps will include the time frame (week, month, quarter, or semester), the content or skill, and the standard taught. Other items that can be included in a curriculum map include essential questions, vocabulary words taught, and materials to be used.

There is a need to continually review and revise curriculum maps to ensure that student learning is up-to-date and valuable (Armstrong, Henson, & Savage, 2005). Maps lend guidance in determining what is to be taught and when it should be taught. Teachers then use their professional judgment for determining strategies for how to best teach students a new concept or idea.

LESSON PLANNING

While standards are determined by the state and the curriculum by the school or district, the teacher will most likely be responsible for writing his/her own lesson plans with learning objectives, and those objectives should incorporate key knowledge and skills from the state standards.

When deciding how to teach the learning objectives, make sure to have a lesson plan. No matter how smart or creative a teacher is, it will only end in disaster if he/she doesn't have a plan as to what to teach, how to teach it, what activities to include, and how much time each activity will take. Many

What Are You Going to Teach Them?

Timeline	Content	Concepts	Processes	Assessments
	Characteristics of Organisms The learner will recognize must meet basic needs to survive. **S-P-LS-1** The learner will identify various structures and functions of plants and animals used in growth and animals used in growth, survival and reproduction and classify these accordingly. **S-P-LS-3**	Flowering/non-flowering (flowers, cones, fruit) Amphibians Human Birds Mammals Insects Spiders	Recognize flowering plants produce seed in a fruit Recognize some plants don't have flowers Classify animals according to their characteristics Plant and animal behavior results from internal and external stimuli	TTP Relationship Report for Life Science POS 1 TTP Relationship Report for Life Science POS 3 TTP Relationship Report for Life Science POS 2
	Life Cycles of Organisms The learner will identify and illustrate life cycles of given organisms. **S-P-LS-5** The learner will recognize offspring resemble their parents. **S-P-LS-4**	Stages of flowering plant (seed, embryo, seedling, adult) Plant seeds Life cycle of non-flowering (moss, fern) (seed/spore, seedling, adult) Life cycle of insect (3 stage: egg, nymph, adult) (4 stage: egg, larva, pupa, adult) Amphibian Bird Mammal	Sequence—draw stages of growth in flowering/non-flowering plants Identify how plants make seeds Compare/contrast flowering and nonflowering plants Illustrate life cycle of a given organism Identify amphibian as a 3 stage (egg, larva, adult)	TTP Relationship Report for Life Science POS 5 TTP Relationship Results for Life Science POS 4

Figure 3.1 Sample Curriculum Map. Retrieved June 2012 from http://www.education.ky.gov/KDE/Instructional+Resources/Curriculum+Documents+and+Resources/ Teaching+Tools/ Curriculum+Maps/

teachers find out the hard way that if they don't use the class time wisely, the students will find a way to use it unwisely. Good planning in most cases leads to good classroom management.

When designing a lesson, teachers should take the following items into consideration: the background knowledge, the objective (or learning goal), the sequence (or learning progression), the learning strategies (or activities), the scaffolds, and the assessment for (and of) learning.

Background knowledge. Discussed deeper in chapter 10, background knowledge, sometimes referred to as prior knowledge, is crucial when learning new skills or concepts. When one learns something new, the mind makes sense of it by attaching the new concept to some prior knowledge. For example, one really can't understand the concept of a waiting room without understanding the concept of a doctor's office or hospital. When one cannot identify with a new concept or new knowledge, one easily becomes confused or jumbled by new terms or ideas. When this occurs, only a small fraction of the new concept is retained in working memory and the brain does not know enough about the new concept to decide what's important and worth memorizing (Lemov, Driggs, & Woolway, 2016).

When creating a lesson, ask, "What will the students have to know in order to understand the new concept? How can the teacher make a connection between this new learning and the learners' lives?" A teacher might have to create a short, ten-minute mini-lesson to ensure the class has the crucial background knowledge needed to learn a new concept or skill. Sometimes a few pictures with a short discussion will do the trick. A small amount of time introducing a topic up front may ensure a smoother entry and aid in retention and application for the long term.

The objective or learning goal. When planning a lesson, look at state academic standards for the grade level. Any important concepts or essential facts and skills should be the key focus of the lesson. Plan to explain to the students what they are going to learn; it should not be a surprise (even for science teachers using exploratory methods, the students should have an idea of what they are to explore). When writing objectives for a lesson, ask, "What does the teacher want students to know and be able to do? What is really the point behind this lesson/standard/topic?"

When deciding on the lesson's learning objectives, the teacher should ask the following:

- Are there any high-frequency words (words that are used often) that I need to make sure to explicitly teach in order for my students to grasp the content knowledge?
- Are there any specialized terms (words that are specific to the topic) that I need to make sure to explicitly teach in order for my students to grasp the content knowledge?
- Are there any cross-curricular references (items that tie into other content areas) that I can incorporate into the lesson to help students make connections?

The learning objective should be active. It should reflect an action that the teacher can see, through either expression or action. The learning action needs to be based around the student. The objective starts with the phrase, "The student/students will . . ." followed by a verb that defines the action that the student will perform. For example:

- Students will summarize . . .
- The student will explain . . .
- Students will create . . . .
- The student will compose . . .
- The student will demonstrate . . .

The focus is on the student acting in a manner that is observable and measurable.

The last component of a successful learning objective is the specific content knowledge the student will demonstrate. For example:

- Students will summarize the plot of *Othello*.
- The student will describe the purpose of the *Bill of Rights*.
- Students will write a persuasive paragraph on the topic of teen pregnancy.
- Students will correctly apply the Pythagorean theorem.

The sequence or learning progression. Just as the yearly or semester curriculum has a sequence, so should a lesson. What are the major parts of the objective/standard? How does this connect to information they have already learned? In what order will content be covered? How will it build up so the students achieve the learning objectives of the lesson?

The learning strategies or activities. In the book *How People Learn: Brain, Mind, Experience and School*, the authors state that "transfer [of new knowledge] is affected by the degree to which people learn with understanding rather than merely memorize sets of facts or follow a fixed set of procedures" (Bransford, Brown, Cocking, & National Research Council, 1999). Within the sequence of activities, how will the teacher provide instruction so that the students truly understand a concept? How will the students be involved in their learning? What can the teacher do to help get the students engaged in the topic? Will the lesson include photos, models, charts, drawings, maps, graphs, timelines, or videos? How will the activities support and align with the learning objectives?

The teacher needs to model the new learning, provide time for the class to work with the new learning together, and then, if they are ready, give the class time to master the new learning by themselves. Students may not be ready for the independent learning phase until the next day, the next week, or perhaps longer. Social constructivists hypothesize that for deep learning to take place, the learners make new meaning through social interaction with others. A teacher standing up in front of a class telling students everything he/she knows on a topic does very little for the student to learn a new topic. Never again should a teacher lecture for 40 minutes and then tell the kids to complete a worksheet individually. This is not an example of good teaching!

The scaffolds. Scaffolding means providing some sort of assistance as needed when a child learns a new skill. As the student progresses and the assistance is no longer needed, the scaffold is removed. Scaffolds can help the student process background knowledge and connect it to new concepts (concept maps), organize information (graphic organizers), or take notes (chapter outlines). Other forms of scaffolds will be discussed in chapter 11. When including scaffolds in a lesson plan, the teacher asks these questions: "What can I be ready to do for the students who might struggle with this? What can I have the proficient students work on while I work with the students who don't get it?"

Lev Vygotsky, an early social constructivist, speaks of a condition in the learning process called the zone of proximal development (ZPD). This zone offers opportunities for learning at a level that is just a bit more challenging than students are comfortable tackling alone (Vygotsky, 1962). This creates an actual "challenge" for the students, but it is a challenge that they feel they can achieve because of support from the teacher. The "scaffold" is in place to support them as they continue their learning and growth (Kingore, 2006).

The formative assessment process assessing for learning is used frequently throughout a lesson to gather evidence of learning and to check for understanding. When planning formative assessment opportunities, the teacher should ask, "How will I know if they learned it? What tools will I use to determine that they know it?" The teacher needs to know what strategies or tools he/she will use to measure what the students know and do not know (Heritage, 2010). These strategies and tools should provide data that will help the teacher decide whether instruction was successful or whether some adjustment and reteaching are necessary to ensure all students are learning before moving on to the next lesson. An important aspect of assessment for learning is that students are allowed to act out a skill or demonstrate knowledge at a level that is rigorous and appropriate. In addition, the teacher should provide prompts and feedback to move the learners forward. Refer to chapter 13 for further reading about assessments.

Effective lesson planning does not have to be complicated, and it does not have to be a guessing game. Researchers in the 1980s (Rosenshine, Barak, & Stevens, 1986) compiled a list of effective procedures successful teachers used. Decades later, this list still represents what successful teachers do. This list can be thought of as the key pieces of effective lesson plan design:

- Quickly review the previous learning before beginning a new lesson (recall previous information that can help students grasp the new knowledge).

- State the learning goals of the lesson (post the objectives of the lesson and state them in student-friendly language, provide a reason as to why they need to learn this).
- Present the new material in small, logical steps and provide practice after each step.
- Provide clear and explicit instruction, demonstrations, and feedback.
- Include active practice that includes all students.
- Ask questions, check for understanding, and elicit responses from all students in the form of signaling, talking, writing, and/or performing.
- Guide students during the first practice (make sure they are doing it correctly).
- Provide feedback to help with needed corrections, assistance, and clarification.
- Monitor students during their seat work, observe the progress, and reteach those who need it.

These nine items can be summarized as follows: The teacher uncovers what the class already knows or does not understand about a concept. The teacher models the new learning, assists students as they try the new skills, and monitors the students to gather evidence of learning or misconceptions as they independently try the new skills. The teacher provides useful, timely, and detailed feedback, as well as time for students to use the feedback to improve independent application of the skill. That's effective teaching!

Learning requires repeated exposure to the content or skill. If the teacher teaches a concept only once, the students probably will not remember it. Research shows that the average student needs exposure to something at least four times to really learn it (Rovee-Collier, 1995). Especially when learning a language or new vocabulary, multiple repetitions are needed for students to learn the association between the word and the referent (McMurray, Horst, & Samuelson, 2012). For a classroom example, repeated reading of a story results in greater average gains in word knowledge (Biemiller & Boote, 2006).

So if the average student needs to be exposed to information at least four times, think about the number of times a struggling student will need exposure. This is why it is important for a teacher to continuously refer back to previous learning, especially within the first few days that the learning was presented.

Exposure to learning content does not always have to come from the teacher; the exposure can also come from the other classmates. This is why it is important to use collaborative activities in pairs or small groups. Also, change up the form of exposure so the students can see and have time to practice the new knowledge in different ways. Examples include offering different examples of well-written topic sentences or providing different angles of an effective free throw. This is called creating "opportunities to learn" (Marzano, Walters, & McNulty, 2005). The more opportunities a student has to learn something, the higher the chance for the student to gain academic success.

REFLECTION SCENARIO

It is summer, and the district has used Title I funds for teachers to meet and develop engaging and authentic mathematics lessons for the next school year. Summative data, benchmark data, and progress monitoring data show third-grade students are struggling with math. The lessons will be designed to increase student academic achievement in math as the teachers integrate the new state standards into the content.

The third-grade team is meeting and planning a geometry unit. Discussion is focused on creating a lesson for the third-grade mathematics domain, Measurement and Data (see the Grade 3 Mathematics Standard below). The grade-level team has come up with a project that will cluster several standards around the essential learning of understanding the concept of area and relating area to multiplication and addition. They have asked the art teacher and a couple of parents to join them in their collaboration.

The team begins the discussion by exploring several questions. How will we know what our students already know about the concept of area? What authentic learning activities will lead to deep understanding? How will we check for understanding (formatively assess) in each of the "I do it, we do it, you do it together, and you do it" phases of the unit. How will we plan for common misconceptions, and what will we have ready to reteach along the way? What other questions would you ask the team to consider that will lead to all students mastering the skills in the standard?

GRADE 3 MEASUREMENT AND DATA DOMAIN

Arizona Academic Standards, 2016

3.MD.C.5 Understand area as an attribute of plane figures and understand concepts of area measurement.

- a. A square with side length 1 unit, called "a unit square," is said to have "one square unit" of area, and can be used to measure area.
- b. A plane figure which can be covered without gaps or overlaps by *n* unit squares is said to have an area of *n* square units.

3.MD.C.6 Measure areas by counting unit squares (e.g., square cm, square m, square in, square ft, and improvised units).

3.MD.C.7 Relate area to the operations of multiplication and addition.

a. Find the area of a rectangle with whole-number side lengths by tiling it, and show that the area is the same as would be found by multiplying the side lengths.
b. Multiply side lengths to find areas of rectangles with whole-number side lengths in the context of solving real-world and mathematical problems, and represent whole-number products as rectangular areas in mathematical reasoning.
c. Use tiling to show that the area of a rectangle with whole-number side lengths a and $b + c$ is the sum of $a \times b$ and $a \times c$. Use area models to represent the distributive property in mathematical reasoning.
d. Understand that rectilinear figures can be decomposed into non overlapping rectangles and that the sum of the areas of these rectangles is identical to the area of the original rectilinear figure. Apply this technique to solve problems in real-world contexts.

3.MD.C.8 Solve real-world and mathematical problems involving perimeters of plane figures and areas of rectangles, including finding the perimeter given the side lengths, and finding an unknown side length. Represent rectangles with the same perimeter and different areas or with the same area and different perimeters.

Arizona 2016 Standards retrieved from: http://www.azed.gov/standards-practices/k-12-standards-feedback/standards-draft-and-public-comments/

Chapter 4

High Expectations and Differentiation

> *What we share in common makes us human. How we differ makes us individuals. In a classroom with little or no differentiated instruction, only student similarities seem to take center stage. In a differentiated classroom, commonalities are acknowledged and built upon, and student differences become important elements in teaching and learning as well . . . Students have multiple options for taking in information, making sense of ideas, and expressing what they learn. In other words, a differentiated classroom provides different avenues to acquiring content, to processing or making sense of ideas, and to developing products.*
>
> —Carol Ann Tomlinson

In one of the author's first year of student teaching, a visiting teacher looked at the roster and proclaimed, "Watch out for Levi. That kid is a pain and should just get expelled already." Thankfully the author did not heed the advice. Although Levi was difficult, with extra time and effort they built a good rapport; Levi learned the material and succeeded in the class.

Charles F. Kettering, the inventor of the electric ignition system and internal lighting in cars, once said, "High achievement always takes place in the framework of high expectations." This concept also applies to teacher expectations of student success. Teachers' beliefs tend to create a self-fulfilling prophecy: teachers will get the outcomes they expect from their students. Take the following scenario as an example:

Jacob is a student in Ms. Ramirez's fourth-grade class. He is often off-task during class and he continually makes excuses for not having his homework. During a review activity for an upcoming test, Ms. Ramirez noticed that Jacob was not engaged. "Of course, he will fail this test," she thinks to herself as she walks past Jacob and moves on to help other students with raised hands.

Consciously and unconsciously, teachers often act and react differently toward students based on the assumptions they have about the individual learner's capabilities. Sociologists call this *symbolic interactionism.* A core tenet of symbolic interactionism is that individuals act toward people and things based on the meanings or feelings that they have given to those people or things (Blumer, 1969). For example, teachers tend to use more validating nonverbal mannerisms such as smiling, creating eye contact, and providing positive body language toward students they believe are high achievers, and use fewer validating mannerisms toward students who they believe are low learners (Bamburg, 2004).

Studies show that low expectations tend to go hand-in-hand with low-achieving classrooms (Cotton, 2001). In these classrooms, teachers generally view students as limited in their ability to learn, and this view creates an atmosphere of failure. These low expectations can be based on past experience, such as assuming that a student's past behavior is predictive of his/her future behavior or making assumptions about current students who share similar characteristics with difficult students from previous years. They are also sometimes based on empathy; the teacher, with the best of intentions, feels for a student because he/she is so far behind. The teacher creates a vicious cycle by going easy on a struggling student instead of increasing the intensity of instruction to help the student meet expectations; giving less work to the student who needs more instruction causes the student to fall further behind. Although empathy is a necessary trait of all effective teachers, educators must be aware of their reactions to these empathetic moments. Finally, many teachers have low expectations because they do not have the tools to create an environment for high expectations.

Conversely, research also shows that when teachers increase their expectations of student success, academic gains are made (Good, 1987). This is known as the "Pygmalion Effect," which means students will produce what is expected of them. If the teacher's mindset is "All students in my class will learn this," they most likely will.

There are strategies that teachers can apply to their daily activities to ensure all students are being held to high expectations, especially those who are thought to be at risk of failure. Include these strategies routinely:

- *Stay away from unreliable "hearsay" about students and their ability to learn.* Focus on the data, not what other students or teachers say.
- *Communicate to students that they have the ability to meet high expectations.* The more often the teacher affirms the student's ability to learn, the more likely the student will try to meet the class goals.

- *Concentrate on offering genuine encouragement and support to all students.* Some students will be receptive and some will not, but continually encourage all students, even the ones who make it seem painful. Provide a double dose of encouragement for at-risk students, and share this encouragement with their family members on a regular basis.
- *Lastly and most importantly, differentiate instruction.* The most critical tool in communicating high expectations is differentiation. Differentiation shows the students that the teacher knows they can get to where they need to be and is willing to help them get there.

PLANNING FOR DIFFERENTIATION OF INSTRUCTION

Differentiation of instruction is shaping instruction to meet the mixed needs of the students. Carol Ann Tomlinson, one of the main authorities on this topic, defines differentiation as a way to "match instruction to student need with the goal of maximizing the potential of each learner in a given area" (Tomlinson & Eidson, 2003). When thinking about differentiation of instruction, use the analogy of getting into a house: the easiest way into a house is through the most traditional means (the front door), but if that doesn't work, there are other ways into the house, such as a back door, window, or chimney. Be prepared to offer alternative teaching methods for children who do not learn in a traditional manner.

Does this mean that an educator needs to teach a concept in 30 different ways for 30 different students? No. It means that the teacher needs to monitor student learning and provide an alternative approach for those who need extra practice, a different explanation, or an advanced assignment to remain interested. It also means that the teacher needs to be *proactive* and plan flexible instructional arrangements within the lesson plan.

Tomlinson identifies four student traits to take into consideration when promoting successful differentiation in the classroom (Tomlinson, 2003):

- *Readiness*—"A student's knowledge, understanding, and skill related to a particular sequence of learning"
- *Interest*—"Topics or pursuits that evoke curiosity and passions in a learner"
- *Learning profile*—"How students learn best"
- *Affect*—"How students feel about their work and the classroom as a whole"

Once these traits are taken into consideration, there are three areas in the curriculum where differentiation can take place (Tomlinson & Allan, 2000): content (what is being taught), process (how the content is taught), and product (how the student will be assessed). Some strategies commonly used for differentiating instruction, for students who are struggling as well as for students who are advanced, include curriculum compacting, learning centers, flexible groupings, delayed wait time, prompting, chunking and checking, tiered assignments, and independent study.

COMPACTING

Compacting consists of eliminating the reiteration of class work that has already been mastered, which can be boring and frustrating for advanced learners, and creating new lessons that the students will find interesting and rigorous (Renzulli, Joseph, & Smith, 1978). The process for compacting consists of certain steps:

1. Select the learning objectives for a given lesson.
2. Use a pretest to assess the class to determine which parts of the lesson students have mastered.
3. Identify students who have mastered the objectives or who might master them at a faster pace than the rest of the class based on the pretest results.
4. Streamline practice and instructional time for students who have already mastered the content.
5. Create enrichment options for eligible students.
6. Keep records of the process and instructional options available to students whose curriculum has been compacted for reporting to parents, and forward these records to next year's teachers.

LEARNING CENTERS

Learning centers provide areas around the classroom where students can work simultaneously on different tasks based on a similar topic. Learning centers can also be used as enrichment tools for students who finish assignments early. These centers must be very organized and preplanned by the teacher to be effective; norms and discipline procedures should be discussed as a whole class to keep disruptions at a minimum. Centers should change from theme to theme to complement the specific topics covered in the lessons. The centers should be focused, meaningful, and engaging to the student.

FLEXIBLE GROUPINGS

Grouping is a common classroom learning activity, and flexible grouping is a strategy for differentiation that is based on specific student needs. Flexible grouping usually starts with whole-group instruction, and then based on checking for the mastery of content, the teacher creates temporary groups based on the need to review, practice, reteach, or enrich.

Flexible grouping allows advanced students to work on engaging and authentic learning, while those who need review or more practice are not left behind. Grouping is flexible because groups will change according to student needs for the specific lesson, and groups can be based on readiness, interest, reading or skill level, background knowledge, or social adequacy. Remember: flexible grouping should only be temporary! The groups should be based on student need and should change depending on the task at hand. See chapter 8 for more information about student grouping.

DELAYED WAIT TIME

All students need "wait time" to process questions before providing answers, but some students will need even more time. For some students, such as students who are hard of hearing, second-language learners, or those who have cognitive disabilities, the teacher will need to provide more time to process information. The length of time that wait time needs to be extended depends on the student or the task at hand. The teacher needs to remain calm and reassure the student that it is okay to take his/her time to respond.

PROMPTING

Prompting, also referred to as cueing, is anything the teacher does to increase the chance the student will get the correct answer. It is similar to giving the student a hint. Prompting can be accomplished through a gesture (such as pointing to a place on a map), demonstration, picture, or sound. However, a student should not become overreliant on prompts, so these should be used minimally or with a plan to eventually remove the prompt as the student progresses.

CHUNK AND CHECK

Chunk and check is a method of breaking content into smaller, organized units and then checking for student understanding before continuing to the next chunk of content. Information should be chunked into sections that can be learned in small steps and with simple instructions. Instructions should be succinct and logical. The teacher should speak clearly, directly, and patiently to the student when explaining the chunk of information. Use examples and modeling techniques and allow time for the student to process the learning.

When checking for understanding, ask the student open-ended questions and prompt the student to explain his/her thinking. Provide feedback to explicitly illuminate what is correct and to clarify what is not correct. Once the student has shown understanding with the first chunk of information, explicitly show how the second chunk of information connects to the first, and the chunk and check method repeats until the student grasps the entire lesson.

TIERED ASSIGNMENTS

Crafting tiered assignments consists of providing the same content to students but varying the assignments based on ability/challenge levels. Even though the assignments are tiered, they should be *equally* challenging for the students and should meet grade-level standards. Differentiation is not appropriate if most students are required to write a report about the impact of the Civil War while one student draws a picture of a horse. In her book *Differentiating Instruction in the Regular Classroom: How to Reach and Teach All Learners,* Diane Heacox provides six ways to structure tiered assignments:

- *Challenge level*—Use Bloom's Taxonomy, discussed in chapter 13, to guide the task at different levels of challenge.
- *Complexity*—Although students may be working on the same assignment, the teacher varies the complexity of the assignment based on the student's level of mastery. As educational author Marian Small states, "Take the same big idea but have different levels of difficulty, thus taking into account the variation in student readiness" (Small, 2010).
- *Resources*—The teacher varies the resources used by reading levels and the complexity of the grade-level standard content.
- *Outcome*—Although students may use the same resources, the outcome may be more advanced for advanced learners.
- *Process*—Although the outcome may be the same for all students, the teacher shows a simpler process for students needing more assistance and requires advanced learners to reach the same outcome through a more difficult process.
- *Product*—The teacher can assign various products to be assessed (Heacox, 2007).

INDEPENDENT STUDY

Independent study provides a student an opportunity to independently work on a project of interest while meeting the goals of the overall lesson. Before any independent study takes place, the teacher and student must agree upon a documented list of outcomes and clear expectations for the project. In many schools, an independent study contract is created and signed by the teacher and student. This contract lists the assignment expectations.

IMPLEMENTING DIFFERENTIATION

Even though differentiation of instruction is included in the lesson plan, the teacher needs continual feedback from students while teaching the lesson. Based on the feedback, ad hoc differentiation strategies, such as flexible groups, can be implemented as needs present themselves. For example, a teacher explains to the class the concept of a verb. The teacher then asks the class to copy a sentence that is written on the board and point to the verb. The teacher walks around the classroom, and as the students write and point, she notices that five students are not pointing at the verb. Based on this data, the teacher changes her approach and differentiates instruction. After assigning each student a partner, she directs each pair to find verbs in their story book. The teacher then brings a small group of students to her desk to work on the exercise with her additional support. Based on her assessment, the teacher has now improvised differentiated instruction for the struggling students by utilizing flexible groupings.

Differentiation creates an atmosphere in which the teacher and students have a sense of a learning community (Tomlinson, 2003). Effective teachers deploy a variety of differentiated instruction strategies in their classrooms daily while holding all students to high expectations.

REFLECTION SCENARIO

During a parent-student-teacher conference early in the school year, the parent of a gifted student brought up how her son, Sam, was disengaged from learning and reported feeling bored with assignments in Ms. Parker's seventh-grade social studies class. The family has traveled widely and made it a point to research future destinations with their children before they visit new countries or regions. This prompted Ms. Parker to reflect on her practice of a one-size-fits-all approach. What could she do to reengage Sam and provide for other students who might already come in knowing the content of a particular unit of study from the standards-based curriculum?

Chapter 5

Supporting School and Classroom Climate

Safety is something that happens between your ears, not something you hold in your hands.

—Jeff Cooper

It is the responsibility of every adult . . . to make sure that children hear what we have learned from the lessons of life, and to hear over and over that we love them and they are not alone.

—Marian Wright Edelman

School improvement is an ongoing goal that affects every school in the nation, no matter what label or status applies. Every school is continually trying to do better than it did the year before. One way to ensure that learning and improvement efforts will continue is by creating and maintaining a healthy school climate. Research shows a direct link between a school's success and the presence of an optimistic, nurturing climate (MacNeil & Maclin, 2005).

Students' lives outside of school can be filled with challenges such as gangs, poverty, and abuse, just to name a few, and these influences can affect the climate of the school. Teaching and learning can be difficult to achieve in an unhealthy school climate. So what can an individual teacher do to contribute to a healthy school climate that supports teaching and learning? Of course, creating a safe and supportive learning environment at the classroom level, through effective classroom management (see chapter 2) and challenging, enriching curriculum (see chapters 3 and 4), is a start, but there are ways that teachers can affect school climate beyond their own classroom.

Many school districts and states have tools to help schools and teachers assess school climate and make improvements. For example, the California

Department of Education and WestEd Regional Comprehensive Center have created the *Workbook for Improving School Climate and Closing the Achievement Gap* (2015), one of the research-based resources that California used together with its Healthy Kids Survey (CHKS) and California School Climate Survey (CSCS) (2015) to help schools develop a positive climate through collaboration among all stakeholders. The *Workbook* identifies eight basic environmental needs: safety, professional learning, cultural responsiveness, school connectedness, teacher quality and retention, student engagement, family involvement, and healthy development (see Figure 5.1).

At the core of these environmental needs are three interrelated factors: caring relationships, high expectations, and opportunities for meaningful participation. Schools that are successful in providing learning environments rich in these three factors are more successful in narrowing achievement gaps.

CARING RELATIONSHIPS

Teachers can contribute to a healthy and positive school climate by establishing positive relationships with students and colleagues. The National Longitudinal Study of Adolescent Health, a study of 90,000 middle and high

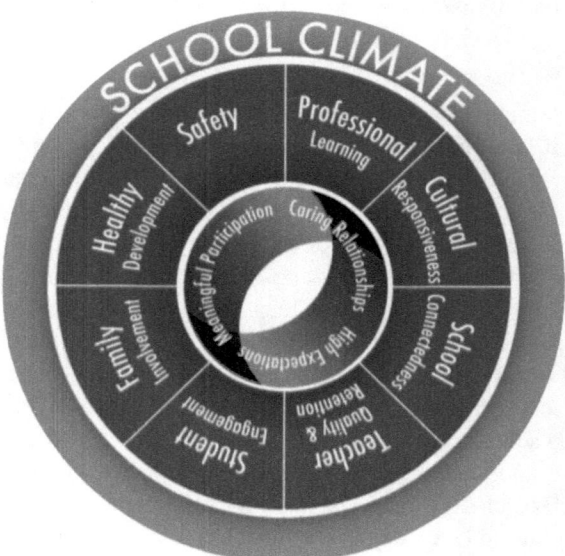

Figure 5.1   From WestEd: West Comprehensive Center (2015). Workbook for Improving School Climate and Closing the Achievement Gap. Retrieved from https://www.wested.org/online_pubs/WB_1221_allv5.pdf

school students, found that students who have strong and quality relationships with teachers were more likely to have better academic achievement, behavior, and attitude (Harris, Udry, Muller, & Reyes, 2010). These students were also less likely to use drugs, commit suicide, join gangs, or show other at-risk behaviors.

Teachers can build a rapport with students by being a positive, nonjudgmental role model whether they are in the classroom, elsewhere on campus, or even out in the community. They can maintain a positive approach in all communications with students, including feedback on assignments. They can make themselves available to students by leaving their door open during lunch and prep periods and having a presence in the hallways during passing periods.

For example, when one of the authors taught high school, a student named Angel was a well-known gang member and disturbance in the school. Although the author was not able to change his lifestyle, they were able to build a relationship with each other. After a year and many, many conversations, Angel toned down his gang presence in school. Because they built a respectful relationship, Angel understood that the author had a job to do and Angel's actions were making that job difficult.

In addition to establishing positive relationships with all students, teachers can promote positive relationships among students and their peers. Well-designed collaborative classroom activities can help students form strong relationships that promote their learning. In addition, the teacher's vigilance in identifying students who seem withdrawn and referring them to appropriate support systems when necessary (guidance counselors, intervention teams) help to promote a sense of safety and belonging (Poynor & O'Malley, 2015).

Teachers can help keep students interested in school by providing a challenging and engaging curriculum. Engaged students tend to have better school attendance and lower dropout rates (Finn, 1989; Mastrorilli, 2016). Students are most motivated to learn, and display the sense of success and achievement, when they are able to succeed at tasks that they find interesting and widening of their capacities.

For example, a high school teacher in Arizona used Clive Barker horror novels to engage a group of eleventh-grade students who were in an alternative program for potential dropouts. After assessing that the students had the ability to complete the assignments but chose not to out of boredom, the teacher made a connection between Clive Barker and Edgar Allan Poe, which led to the students reading classic literature and writing a literature analysis comparing the two authors.

Finally, teachers can establish caring relationships with their colleagues through collaboration and participation in learning communities. Participation in school teams that develop a school safety plan, discipline code, and/or mission statement for the school not only empowers teachers to have an influence on school policies, but also enables them to learn from colleagues. Collaboration provides opportunities for colleagues to talk to one another about what they are doing to build better relationships with students and families.

HIGH EXPECTATIONS

Remember that teachers are role models. Teachers must model the behavior expected from students and consider this as important as the teaching of academic standards. A teacher might be the only "responsible citizen" the student interacts with. It is important to show how a responsible adult acts. This can include how a responsible person acts when frustrated, how a responsible person acts when mad, how a responsible person acts when disappointed, or even how a responsible person acts when faced with conflict.

As a role model, the teacher needs to show and discuss the successes that can be achieved by getting an education. Certainly, one way is by sharing with the students how important education is and the requirements of professional certification and continuing education for teachers and for principals. Holding career days, providing mentoring programs, and inviting other professionals in to discuss the role and power of education in their lives are other ways to build, celebrate, and model a culture of learning. For a culture of learning to exist in a school, positive, productive behavior needs to reign.

Several nonprofit character education programs are available, such as The Be Kind People Project (2017) and Character Counts (2015). The Be Kind People Project has the vision of building a generation of respectful, responsible, and caring citizens and leaders. This skill set, which can be an integral part of lifelong decision making, can be practiced in the school and classroom environment. The Association of American Educators site (2017) lists several more character education programs that have proven and recommended curricula. These groups provide programs that promote positive school culture and climate for today's schools.

OPPORTUNITIES FOR MEANINGFUL PARTICIPATION

One of the most effective methods for creating a positive school climate is to provide ways for all students to be involved in the school. When students find a meaningful role in their school, they are less likely to engage in disruptive behavior than students who feel out of place and excluded. Teachers can help promote meaningful participation by encouraging student participation in extracurricular activities.

Remember to reward good behavior instead of only punishing students for unacceptable behavior. Positive messages need to outweigh negative messages. For at-risk students, try to provide a 4:1 ratio of positive message to negative message.

FAMILY INVOLVEMENT

Research shows that parent involvement can assist in improving student achievement (Epstein, 1987; Poynor & O'Malley, 2015; National Parent Teacher Association, 2017). While administrators are responsible for developing school-wide initiatives to involve families, individual teachers can also do their part.

Teachers can include parents by trying to meet with them at least twice a year face-to-face during parent-student-teacher conferences or orientation nights, provide materials or suggestions about how parents can assist their children at home, and contact the parents when the student is having problems or has accomplished successes. Although society as a whole should be trying to increase all forms of a parent involvement in a child's life, the key role for the teacher is to find a way to link the parent or family member to the student's learning.

Based on the comfort level of the parent, parental involvement can be something as minimal as verbally expressing to their child that they have academic expectations or asking about what they learned in school, or can include something as substantial as providing after-school tutoring or volunteering to assist as a teacher aide. In some charter schools, parents sign up for a suggested yearly number of volunteer hours in the school at the time of registering their students.

Another important thing to remember is that some cultural, educational, and language issues can become barriers to parental involvement. A report by the California Department of Education stated that schools must actively acknowledge and respect parents' culture while informing them of the way the American education system works and opportunities that are available for parent involvement (Ramirez & Douglas, 1989).

Parents who had a bad experience in school or even dropped out might feel intimidated by an academic setting or feel like they have nothing to offer. These parents can assist teachers by merely

- asking their child about his/her school day and what was taught in the class;
- making sure a quiet place and time are available for homework;

- scheduling a healthy time for the child to go to bed and wake up during the school week; and
- talking to the child about the importance of education and post–high school opportunities, including college.

Teachers can also include parents by not unintentionally excluding them. For example, a school could be making a concerted effort to use academic vocabulary and make the students speak in proper, complete sentences. When students speak improperly, teachers correct them by saying things like, "No, speak like you're educated" or "Educated people don't talk like that." An unintended consequence of this could be students going home and telling their family that they speak like they are uneducated or stupid. As a consequence, parents and the community could feel unwelcome and even spiteful toward the school. The teachers and administration could change their response to "Because this is a school, we will speak academic English within the building. At home or with your friends you can decide the best way to communicate." By simply changing this to a positive message, the teachers and school are not unintentionally excluding members of the community. This also provides a reminder of how fragile the school-community partnership can be.

As a teacher who wants to get families more involved in school, start by finding out what the school's administration and teachers consider "family involvement" as well as examples of opportunities within the school for families to get involved. Remember to take into consideration the students in the class who have a guardian such as a grandparent, an aunt, or an uncle in the parent role. There has been a shift in thinking to add the term *family engagement* when talking about parent involvement. Whatever terms and common understanding of family involvement are in place, if a program does not exist, find out if leadership is willing to gather resources to start one.

The Parent Institute (Wherry, 1996) offers these suggestions for getting parents involved in the classroom:

- Help parents understand they are the most important teacher in their child's life. It is said that from birth until high school graduation, children will spend 15 percent of their time at school and 85 percent of their time at home. Politely explain to parents that they are the most influential educator to their child and that their views on education will affect their child's view on education.
- Provide a list of ways parents can help in the classroom or with their child's education. In some cultures, parents would never think about interfering with the school. Let parents know they are welcome to assist, and provide various opportunities in which they might be able to lend a hand.

- Keep it brief when sending information home. Keep it to one page in length and use a sixth-grade reading level. The longer the request, the lower the chance parents will read it. Send communications frequently, but keep them short.
- Have a plan. A teacher should not ask for parent assistance and then have no plan for parents to help.
- Thank them! Always go out of the way to send a card or an e-mail, even after thanking them personally. Parents are busy, so make sure they really understand the difference they made!

For more resources, Poynor and O'Malley (2015) developed the *Climate Connection Toolkit: Low- and No-Cost Activities for Cultivating a Supportive School Climate*. This evidence-based resource supports the school climate and safety program designed for California schools; however, it can be used by any school. The tool addresses and includes topics from the briefs that came out of the WestEd/California School Climate and Safety Program research. Suggestions include:

- Find out the communication preference for different families (in person, e-mail, phone, or text message).
- Provide families with teacher e-mail addresses so they can ask questions.
- Communicate with families about their children's strengths.
- Share good news promptly and through the family's preferred method of communication.
- Avoid correcting mistakes in family members' written or spoken language.

REFLECTION SCENARIO

Your principal asks each grade level to host a meeting for their parents to teach parents how to understand their child's data, from student portfolios and progress monitoring data to proficiency test results. How would you plan the meeting? What is your agenda for the night? What support would you need from your district and principal? What are some strategies to ensure a good parent turn-out? What would be your follow-up during the year?

Chapter 6

Student Mobility and Attendance

Those who get lost on the way to school will never find their way through life.

—German Proverb

The only real security that a man can have in this world is a reserve of knowledge, experience and ability.

—Henry Ford

If students are not present in class, it is very difficult for them to learn what is being taught. The more a student is absent, the more he/she falls behind, and the more difficult it is for the teacher to help the student "catch up." Poor attendance creates gaps and a lack of continuity in a child's learning, and it increases the chances that the child will eventually drop out of school. Common causes of poor student attendance fall into four categories (Baker, Sigman, & Nugent, 2001):

1. *Family.* Sometimes families do not value education or are not aware of the importance of being in school on a daily basis. Sometimes the family structure is dysfunctional (drugs, lack of supervision), which hinders a child's ability to get to school.
2. *School.* Issues related to an unhealthy or unsafe school environment, such as bullying, teacher attitudes, or class size, can cause students to not want to attend.
3. *Economics.* The cost of transportation or the necessity to have a job can limit a student's ability to regularly attend school.

4. *Ability to learn.* Emotional and physical health issues will create attendance issues. Also, if a student is struggling to keep up with the class, the chance of truancy increases.

Most attendance policies will be created at a school or district level. Teachers should be familiar with these policies so that they can provide timely and appropriate interventions. Ideally, the school or district will have procedures for identifying, contacting, and counseling chronically absent students. Most schools will try to contact these students first by phone, then through e-mail, and then with a home visit. To promote attendance, some schools and districts will provide incentives, such as rewards or parties for the students with good attendance. Incentives like these tend to favor the students who are already consistently attending class but do little for the students who are already missing school, especially at the high school level.

What can a teacher do to keep attendance up in class? First, rather than providing rewards for good attendance, the teacher can make showing up for class the reward for all students by providing engaging instruction and learning activities in daily lesson plans. The more students are engaged, the more they'll want to attend the class. Once students are disengaged, the chance they will miss school increases, especially in high school. It is just human nature; people are attracted to things they enjoy or find exciting, and they avoid things that are boring or stressful or that seem unachievable.

Another essential practice is for the teacher to regularly monitor attendance and intervene when a student's attendance becomes a problem. If a student is persistently absent, do not punish him/her since there can be many reasons that influence attendance that are beyond the student's control. Punishment is rarely an effective strategy. Ask the student privately why he/she missed so many classes. Based on the answer, the teacher or school counselor might assist the student with the challenges that are preventing regular attendance. The option of after-school or before-school tutoring can be used to compensate for the time the student has missed.

Communication with the student's family is also essential for addressing attendance difficulties at both the elementary and the secondary levels. When contacting a family member, a phone call is usually the first step. In this conversation, state the number of times the student has been absent, explain that the student's presence has been missed, and give details about what the class has learned while the student was out. Make sure to emphasize that the student's lack of attendance is noticed and his/her participation is missed.

In addition, ask the parent/guardian if there is anything the school, not just the teacher, can do to assist in getting the child to school. Based on the answer, decide whether there is a practical solution and contact the school administrator if needed. The problem could be as simple as, "Sarah feels intimidated by Thomas and has not been wanting to attend since the new seating chart was implemented," in which case the teacher has a lot of control over the solution. The problem might also be as difficult as, "Our family car has been repossessed and we have no way of getting her to school unless her aunt picks her up," and a school counselor or administrator should be contacted to assist in finding a solution.

If the phone call does not help improve student attendance, talk to the school counselor or principal about a home-based intervention. Do not do a home-based intervention without consulting the school's counselor, nurse, social worker, or principal first! Due to safety reasons and a possibly delicate situation, the school principal or other appropriate personnel should be brought into the conversation. These home-based interventions can address issues such as transportation, housing arrangements, sleep schedules, homework times, truancy laws, etc. Again, these interventions shouldn't seem like a scolding or a punishment; they should be used as a positive way to increase the parent's awareness of the situation and the student's ability to get to school.

STUDENT MOBILITY

Student mobility, or the unscheduled moving of a student from school to school, is a prevalent problem across the United States and is the cause of many students not attending school regularly. During an average K–12 education in the United States, approximately 31 percent of students changed school once, 34 percent twice, 18 percent three times, and 13 percent four or more times prior to starting high school (Feil, Haskins, & Turley, 2013). Unfortunately, these frequent changes are directly linked to low attendance, lack of achievement, poor test scores, and even referrals for special education services (Alexander, Entwisle & Dauber, 1996; Boon, 2011; Parke & Kanyongo, 2012; Sparks, 2016).

Mobility tends to affect some subgroups more than others. The majority of students who suffer from mobility are from the inner-city or high-poverty homes, with some urban schools claiming student turnover rates as high as 80 percent (Stover, 2000). Second-language learners also tend to have a high mobility rate. On average, economically disadvantaged students tend to struggle more academically, so a high rate of mobility adds to the chance of a downward academic spiral. A study of 10,000 high school students showed that mobility between the first and eighth grade for *all* types of students increases the odds of becoming a dropout (Stover, 2000).

Some states have a higher mobility rate than others as well as different types of mobility. Colorado and Missouri have more urban mobility, while Nebraska, Wyoming, and Arizona see more rural mobility. The mobility in a distant, rural locale might occur for different reasons than the mobility of an inner-city school. Smaller mining towns might have a continually mobile population as old mines close and new mines open (Fong, Bae, & Huang, 2010). Most mobility "hot spots" have poverty above the state's mean, and the mobility occurs when parents have to move when trying to find work or when losing their current housing situation.

Poverty and the economy have enormous effects on student mobility. States such as Arizona and California have seen people leave as the housing market crumbled.

Mobility that crosses state lines affects student learning due to differences in academic standards. Although some states may have the same academic grade requirements as other states, this is not always the case as the United States does not have national standards or graduation requirements. Per federal law (Every Student Succeeds Act), each state is responsible for student learning. This means some states may have higher standards for students than other states. For students moving from one state to another, this can cause a disruption in learning since the content the student was learning at the previous school could be significantly harder or easier at the new school depending on the academic rigor of that state's standards.

Based on the Programme for International Student Assessment (PISA), a triennial international survey to evaluate international education systems, top-performing countries utilized national standards, with the exception of Canada, where each of the ten provinces is responsible for creating its own standards. In 2016, the United States ranked 25th out of 70 participating countries (OECD, 2016).

Most mobile students go through inter-district transfers, meaning that they leave a school from one district and go to another school in another district. No matter the size of the school or district, it is hard to keep records "clean" or accessible if the population is very mobile. This makes it hard for a teacher to use past records to assess where a student is academically and know what supports were previously in place. Teachers need to be proactive when new students join their classes so that they can be sure to support those students and help them be successful in school.

Here are some suggestions for teachers to help reduce the impact of mobility on a student's learning as well as promote the student's socialization in the new learning environment:

- Speed up the process of integrating a student into a class as much as possible.
- Create "buddy systems" by partnering new students with current, productive students. This will increase the student's role in the class and help the student feel accepted.

- Make a follow-up appointment with parents two weeks after the student transfers into the class to discuss how their child is adjusting.
- Know the resources and outreach programs that your school or district offers to educate parents about minimizing the negative effects of mobility so that you can refer them when necessary. The more parents are educated about how student mobility can decrease student achievement, the more parents will try to find ways to keep their child in the current school or school district.
- If the change in schools is inevitable, offer guidance to resolve any problems that are causing the student to want to transfer and urge the parents to keep their children in the same school for at least the remainder of the school year.

REFLECTION SCENARIO

James has been absent three days this week, and he has a history of extended absences. His sixth-grade teacher phoned James's house and found that his mother had asked him to stay home to watch his brother, a third grader, who is home with the flu. The mother is a single parent and must work two jobs to support the family. How would you handle the situation? Are there students in your school who have had absentee issues? What is your district's policy regarding absenteeism?

Chapter 7

Time on Task

The most successful man in life is the man who has the best information.

—Benjamin Disraeli

An average student in the United States spends around 179 days in school, but how much of that time is actually spent learning? This has been a question of interest for decades. A 1983 study showed that only 60 percent of the school day was spent on instruction and that girls spent more time engaged in learning than boys (Rossmiller, 1983). A few years later another study presented scarier statistics, showing that only half of the school day focused on actual instruction (Honzay, 1986). A 2003 study painted an even more dismal picture: students spent only about 42 percent of their school day engaged in learning (Martella, Nelson, & Marchand-Martella, 2003).

Excitingly, a 2013 study indicated that elementary school students are focused on learning close to 70 percent of the time (Godwin, Almeda, Petroccia, Baker, & Fisher, 2013). In an era in which students will be competing for jobs in a global market, it is crucial that time in class is fully and effectively utilized. By increasing the opportunities for students to learn, also called *time on task*, the teacher is increasing the opportunities for the students to succeed.

Time on task is crucial to student learning, especially in cognitively demanding classes, such as mathematics or foreign languages (Brewster & Fager, 2000). The more time students are engaged in a subject, the more deeply they will comprehend it. So what are some things that can cause time *off* task? Here are a few items guaranteed to disrupt instructional time:

1. *Lack of a plan.* Making stuff up "on the fly" wastes instructional time. Without a plan, students will be confused, the teacher will be explaining things over and over, and time will be lost. Remember that great teachers model what they expect from their students. If students are expected to be prepared to learn, then teachers need to be prepared to teach.
2. *Bird walking.* Bird walking is a nice way of saying "getting off topic." All teachers have a subject or hobby they love to talk about. A Spanish teacher could ramble on about a summer vacation to Spain. While brief, personal stories that are relevant to the learning can help enhance engagement, swaying off topic wastes instructional time. Teachers need to make sure the majority of time with students is focused on the intentional learning, not other trivial topics.
3. *No structure.* As explained in chapter 1, structure is crucial to effective teaching. Without structure in a class, the teacher will spend more time organizing chaos than actually teaching students the necessary content.

In order to increase time on task within the classroom, educators should begin to focus on three factors: well-being, preparation, and curriculum and instruction.

WELL-BEING

A student's physical state influences his/her ability to learn, so it is important that teachers, schools, and districts ensure, to the best of their ability, that every student is properly nourished and ready to learn. Studies have shown that students who eat healthfully perform better on standardized tests and are faster and more accurate in responding to problem-solving tasks (Pollitt, 1991; Belot & James, 2009; Li & O'Connell, 2012). Harvard University and the Massachusetts General Hospital concluded that children who regularly ate breakfast had better behavior and were less hyperactive than children who skipped breakfast (Murphy, Wehler, Pagano, Little, Kleinman, & Jellinek, 1998).

Teachers and principals doing something as simple as providing granola bars or fruit to students can increase the chances that students will spend more time learning in the classroom. If a teacher feels a student does not have a stable home environment that provides food, shelter, and sleep, the teacher should contact the school counselor to find assistance. Many schools have federal or state programs to assist students who cannot afford regular nutritious meals.

As many as one in five school-aged children suffers from some degree of mental illness (Younger, 2017). Because teachers spend so much time with students, it is not rare for a teacher to be the first person to notice abnormal behaviors in a child. Although there are things teachers can do to support students who are internalizing or externalizing problems (such as providing more positive reinforcement, creating a more organized schedule, providing additional time for assignments, or creating a routine for the student to start when feeling angry or anxious), by no means should teachers feel this is an issue they need to deal with alone, as most teachers are not prepared to handle such situations (Sparks, 2016). Teachers who see warning signs that a child might be in need should address the school's policy on this issue or seek assistance from a school administrator, nurse, social worker, or psychologist.

Educators also need to find the time to take care of themselves. Many teachers are altruists who are willing to put the needs of others first. Unfortunately, this can lead to stress. Everyone requires and deserves a little "me" time. Researchers have concluded that educator stress affects the ability to effectively teach and adversely influences the quality of instruction that students receive (Kokkinos, 2007; Skaalvik & Skaalvik, 2007; Aghar, 2008). Teachers need to commit time to enjoy stress-relieving activities outside of the school day.

PREPARATION

As stated earlier, being prepared saves time. It sounds simple, but just as in sports, the team with the best game plan tends to win. When preparing, teachers should ask themselves the following questions:

- What will I be teaching? What success criteria will my students be able to meet to show me they learned it?
- Do I understand the content? If not, what do I need to learn before I teach it?
- In what order will things be taught? What materials are needed? What do the students already know?
- Am I asking them to learn something new? Am I providing them with a rigorous learning experience while still being realistic about what can be accomplished within the timeframe? Are the learning targets and activities appropriate for my students?

The most important thing a teacher can do to increase learning time is clearly state classroom rules and model and reinforce those rules on a consistent basis (Walker, Audette, & Algozzine, 1998; Marzano, 2003). As explained in chapter 2, rules should be concise, easy to understand, and positive. Remember that students help define the rules as well as the consequences for breaking the rules. Teachers need to explain to the students why the rules are in place. If students understand the rationale behind the rules, it is less likely that they will break them (Marzano & Brown, 2009).

Lastly, remember that the way teachers organize their classrooms in preparation for a lesson can increase student engagement and, therefore, increase time on task. As stated in chapter 2, when seating is arranged to address the task at hand (e.g., U-shaped seating arrangement for classroom discussions or rows for test taking), students will remain engaged for a longer period of time (Bonus & Riordan, 1998). Students ask significantly more questions when seated in a semicircle than in rows (Marx, Fuhrer, & Hartig, 2000). A classroom arrangement that is not beneficial to the student or the task at hand can affect student learning by as much as 50 percent (Black, 2007).

ENGAGING CURRICULUM AND INSTRUCTION

Curriculum is a key part of the learning experience and becomes the foundation on which engagement is built (Hunter, 2014). Curriculum should be challenging, yet realistic (Brewster & Fager, 2000). Many student distractions occur when a child is bored or overwhelmed by the curriculum. As discussed in chapter 3, teachers need to be very strategic when planning content and instruction.

Active student engagement in classroom instruction is critical to learning. In classrooms where active participation is required and not an option, work completion and attendance rates increase while behavioral problems are reduced (Voke, 2002). Engagement goes beyond getting students to comply, although compliance must be achieved before students can become engaged in a lesson or an activity, and sometimes just getting students to comply is a winning situation. However, teachers must plan engaging curriculum and instruction to get students "into" or involved in what is being taught. Engaging curriculum incorporates "instructional activities involving students in doing things and thinking about what they are doing" (Bonwell & Eison, 1991). When students think about what they are doing and why they are doing it, the learning becomes purposeful and relevant.

Students will be more engaged in *authentic learning*, learning that relates to their lives and includes real-world situations (Lumsden, 1994). Authentic learning happens when students can directly apply knowledge and skills to current events or situations they find relevant (Fuller, 2013). When students engage in authentic learning, they see school work as pertinent and worthy of their efforts. Creating the connection between what is being learned and how it affects the student in life makes the content engaging to the student.

Another way to engage students is to have them take responsibility for learning. One way to let students take some responsibility is to allow for choices in assignments. For instance, the teacher provides a general topic, such as World War II, and a general due date as well as some nonnegotiable criteria. The students might, within that general topic, pick weaponry, the role of women, famous authors of the time period, famous treaties, etc. The students check in weekly with the teacher for a progress report. If students miss a deadline, the teacher asks them to explain why they missed it and how they will make it up. Empowering the students to make decisions increases their engagement in the assignment. Suddenly, the assignment is personal.

When teachers fail to sufficiently plan for student engagement, they wait until they are struck by blank expressions from ranks of students who appear to be catatonic before reaching into their bag of tricks to grab the students' attention. Many experienced teachers can improvise, but it does take up precious instructional time to react, reflect, choose, and execute a strategy that will eventually save the day. Does it not make more sense to intentionally plan for student engagement from the very beginning?

REFLECTION SCENARIO

In the areas of well-being, preparation, and curriculum and instruction, what are some ways that you can ensure your time will be spent addressing important topics? What are some items that you feel might prevent you from staying on task?

Chapter 8

A Deep Dive in Student Engagement

All men by nature desire knowledge.

—Aristotle

There are two kinds of teachers: the kind that fills you with so much quail shot that you can't move, and the kind that just gives you a little prod behind and you jump to the skies.

—Robert Frost

The amount of external engagement a child receives during the day can be staggering: cell phones, text messaging, Tweets, social media, Google+, vines, Snapchat, FaceTime, Skype, Instagram, streaming video, streaming music, video games, etc. The average teen sends close to 1,000 texts a month, with this number being even higher for girls between the ages of 15 and 17 (Pew Research Center, 2015). Given these circumstances, one cannot expect children to sit still and remain interested in listening to a teacher talk for 50 minutes. Today's students expect information to be fast and can "digest" it in different forms.

Most classroom disruptions don't occur because the "Bart Simpson" in the room was born a trouble maker. Classroom disruptions occur because students are not engaged: Those who do not understand the content would rather be seen as troublemakers than stupid, those who are bored cause trouble as a form of entertainment, and then there is a small portion of students who just want someone to pay attention and they will get that attention any way possible. Engaging students in learning can alleviate all these three issues.

When students are asked to interact or participate, they have less time to daydream, entertain themselves, or cognitively wander off. Also, when students are actually engaged in practicing what they are learning, the teacher can assess if the students are doing it correctly. If a teacher is just lecturing and the students are just listening, it is difficult for the teacher to assess if the students actually understand the content, or if they are really even listening (we all know how easy it is to "act" like we are listening when, in reality, we aren't paying the slightest bit of attention).

Successful student engagement begins with a positive atmosphere for learning. To create a positive atmosphere, teachers must allow enough wait time when expecting an answer to a question, dignify incorrect responses, repeat a question, or give hints that will encourage students to try again (Marzano et al., 1992).

There are four specific attributes of teachers who successfully engage students (Fitterer et al., 2004). The teacher must

- elicit *all* students to be engaged in the learning *at the same time*;
- elicit students to be engaged in the academic learning;
- ensure student engagement is *mandatory* for all students throughout the learning; and
- maintain engagement of all students.

The six basic ways to meet these attributes are having students speak, write, signal, perform, think, or a combination of these ways (Smith, 2009; Fitterer et al., 2004).

Speaking is the ability to talk during the classroom session. When creating lesson plans, teachers must actively create time for students to talk about the content discussed.

Writing is the physical motion of putting thoughts on a page. By stopping to have students write or fill in a graphic organizer, the teacher is engaging the students in the learning process with a physical (although minor) activity.

Signaling is a physical motion to a question or topic. This can be as easy as the students giving a "thumbs up" if they think a statement is correct.

Performing is providing some sort of physical motion to the content. This can include students mimicking the way earth circles the sun or using types of manipulatives.

Thinking is a covert form of engagement that can be provided by the teacher giving students think time to process a certain concept.

Combination refers to two or more of the above being used at the same time.

By including these various ways of engagement into the lesson plan, teachers will be creating an environment where students are being active participants in the learning.

TECHNIQUES TO INCREASE ACTIVE PARTICIPATION

There are many techniques to engage students in creative ways. Below are a handful of techniques that can be used across most grades and content areas.

Choral responses. Choral responses occur when the class as a whole repeats an answer or term out loud and at the same time. Choral responses are best used when the reply is short and exact (Smith, 2009).

When using a choral response, the teacher should ask the question, provide a signal that it is silent think time (e.g., the teacher puts a hand up), and then provide a cue when it is time for the entire class to respond (e.g., the teacher lowers the hand while saying "everyone"). Using the signal and cue for choral response on a regular basis creates a habitual method of active participation in the classroom. There are many opportunities during instruction to use choral response:

- If students are looking at a common stimulus, the teacher can point to the stimulus, ask the question, give think time, and then signal for the response (Archer & Hughes, 2011).
- If students are looking at their own book/paper, the teacher can have the students point to the section in the book being referenced; the teacher asks the question and then uses a signal to elicit the response (e.g., saying "everyone").

Partners. Much research shows that student achievement increases when students are allowed to occasionally work in pairs (Tsui, 1995; Andrews, 2003; Westbrook, 2011; Achmad & Yusuf, 2014). When assigning partners, the teacher creates the partnerships rather than students choosing their partners.

Student grouping can be difficult and should vary depending on the task at hand. For instance, pairing the best reader with the worst reader will only cause frustration for the students and the teacher. A rule of thumb is to begin by privately (not in front of the students) listing the students by achievement for the specific task. Once listed, split the group in the middle and then assign partners. If the class has 30 students, student #1 will pair with student #15, #2 with #16, #3 with #17, etc. This type of grouping provides a knowledge gap between students that is manageable. Each partner should be given a number (1 or 2) and physically sit next to his/her assigned partner (Smith, 2009).

Partners can be used in various ways. The partners can say answers to each other, retell the content of a story, review content, brainstorm, explain processes or strategies, give examples, or even read to each other. Two sets of partners can also be joined to create a larger partnership.

Before using partners, the teacher must explicitly teach students how to work together and how to give and receive encouragement and compliments (Archer & Hughes, 2011). Students need to understand that the partnership is for learning, not friendship, and the teacher should change the partnerships occasionally (every three to six weeks).

Written responses. When having students write, the teacher must make sure that the length of the written response is sufficient to avoid dead time. In other words, make the response fairly short or make the response endless to keep students from wandering off after completion. When completed, the teacher should have students put their pencils down to show completion or turn their paper over.

Other ways to quickly and effectively engage students include the student touching the stimuli (e.g., a sentence in a book) with the pencil, which allows the teacher to monitor each student's attention to the stimuli; acting out or recreating an event recently studied; using hand signals to share categorical responses; and displaying answers with response cards.

Think/pair/write/share. In think/pair/write/share, the teacher asks a higher-order question and then provides time for the students to individually think of a reply. Students then pair with a predetermined partner and discuss their thoughts regarding the question while the teacher wanders the room to assess the student conversations. The students then agree to an answer for the question, write it down, and share it with the larger group.

Think/pair/write/share provides all students the opportunity to discuss a concept and learn from one another (Smith, 2009). In order to effectively implement this strategy, the teacher should follow these steps:

- *Think*—Have students think and record responses. As students are writing, the teacher walks the room and records ideas and names on an overhead transparency, a paper, or a tablet.
- *Pair/write*—Have students share their ideas with their partners. Have them record (write) their partner's best ideas. As students are sharing, the teacher continues to record ideas.
- *Share*—The partners share their ideas with the entire class, or the teacher uses the transparency, paper, or tablet for sharing with the class.

Because their response has a higher chance of being correct after working with a partner, students will be more willing to state it in front of the class.

Think/pair/write/share is a great four-step strategy that ensures all kids can be called upon and provide a thoughtful answer. Let's look at it again within an actual scenario. It starts with the teacher asking a question:

"What are the attributes of a circle? Think about it."

By providing think time or wait time, the teacher is giving the students time to devise a quality answer and make connections between the question and what they know. This will increase the quality of answers as well as class participation.

The rule of thumb is to provide five seconds of wait time, but more complex questions may require more time, while simple questions ("What month is it?") may need only one or two seconds of wait time. For new teachers, wait time can feel awkward and five seconds of silence can seem like a minute. Count the amount of wait time silently and remind students that they are not allowed to blurt answers out until the teacher signals that the wait time is over.

Next, the teacher directs the students to pair up. As stated earlier, students should know who their partner is in the beginning of the lesson.

"Turn to your partner and share your answer. Discuss your ideas. Are there any ideas that you both had? Write them down. If your partner has any new information and you both agree it's correct, write it down as well."

As they pair and share their answers with their partners, the teacher walks around the room to monitor the activity and correct any misconceptions. By having the students share answers with a partner first, the students can safely see if they are "on the same page" and be reassured they have an answer to share if called upon. The teacher can also write down some of the answers provided and share with the group. Once the students have been given adequate time to share, the teacher brings the class back to attention.

"You have five seconds to end your conversation and bring your attention to me. One, two, three . . ."

Once the attention is back on the teacher, the teacher can call on a group to share their answers or state some of the items the he/she heard from the students.

"Excellent job. Suzy and Alfredo said a circle is round. That's correct. If you didn't write that down, please do so now. Jamal and Adam said a circle doesn't have a pointy edge, like a triangle does. This is correct as well. . ."

Think/pair/write/share is a great alternative to randomly calling on students or posing a question and asking students to raise their hands if they know the answer. Think/pair/write/share can also be modified to write/pair/share, read/pair/share, watch/pair/share, or even listen/pair/share. This can be used often within a class and gets many students involved instead of only the "high-flyers" or the "blurters" speaking out and engaging in the lesson.

Choral reading. Choral reading is similar to choral response in that the entire class is reading the same thing at the same time. The teacher notifies the

60   Chapter 8

students where to begin in the text and then reads the selection aloud with the students. The teacher needs to read at a moderate pace and remind students that their volume should be the same as the teacher's.

Cloze reading. In cloze reading (not to be confused with close reading, which is the critical analysis of a text), the teacher reads the passage as the class follows along quietly. The teacher occasionally stops and the class is expected to say the word that comes next out loud (Rye, 1982). The teacher should stop on meaningful words that are crucial to comprehension.

Silent reading. Silent reading occurs when each student reads the passage silently. Before beginning, the teacher should pose a pre-reading question for students to think about while reading. The teacher tells students to read a certain passage and asks them to reread the material if they finish early. Silent reading should be monitored, so the teacher wanders the room as students read silently (Garan & DeVoogd, 2008). The teacher asks individuals to whisper-read to the teacher if the teacher taps their shoulder, and then poses a post-reading question for the class to answer once the silent reading is completed.

Partner reading. With partner reading, the teacher assigns each student a partner (see above for partnering) and then one partner whisper-reads to the other partner. The teacher clarifies that students alternate by sentence, paragraph, page, or length of time.

No matter which technique is used, after the teacher gets the students engaged in the learning, the teacher will need to always monitor and correct, throughout eternity. Usually, teachers who get the best results in their classes are always on their feet, moving around, sitting with students, showing examples, or monitoring small groups while positioning themselves in the classroom where they can see what the rest of the class is doing. Students will learn more, retain more, and remain engaged when they actively participate in the learning (Akey, 2006). When student engagement is alive and well, teacher engagement is also increased and everyone ends each school day with a sense of accomplishment and a feeling of satisfaction.

SAMPLE APPLICATION ACTIVITY—THE JIGSAW

The following example incorporates many of the concepts covered in this chapter. The jigsaw activity has been around for decades and is a useful way to use cooperative learning in all grades as well as with adult learners.

To begin, the teacher breaks the class into smaller groups and the students in each group are numbered. For example, the assignment is to read a chapter and discuss the five parts of a plot. The class is broken into four groups with five students in each group. Each student in the group is given a number (see Figure 8.1).

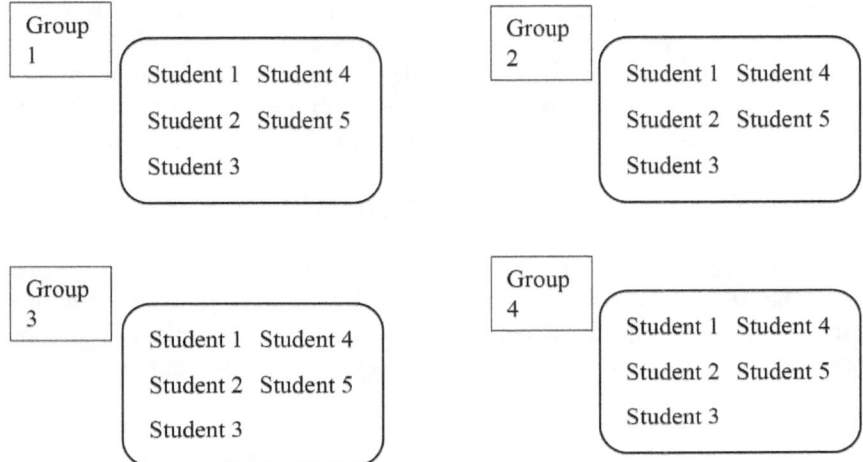

Figure 8.1   Jigsaw Grouping. Adapted from Aronson & Patnoe (1997)

At this point, the teacher assigns each number a task:

"1's will read and take notes about conflict, 2's will read and take notes about rising action, 3's will read and take notes about the climax, 4's will read and take notes about the falling action, and 5's will read and take notes about the resolution."

As the students read, the teacher walks around the room monitoring the class and assisting when needed. Once the students read and take notes on their assigned portion of the assignment, the students with the same assignment from the other groups get together to compare the information:

"All 1's meet in the west corner of the room and compare notes. Make sure you all agree on the most important information. All 2's meet in the east corner of the room and compare notes. Make sure you all agree on the most important information. All 3's meet in the north corner of the room and compare notes. Make sure you all agree on the most important information. All 4's meet in the south corner of the room and compare notes. Make sure you all agree on the most important information. All 5's meet in the center of the room and compare notes. Make sure you all agree on the most important information."

As the students meet and discuss, the teacher monitors the room and assesses each group's understanding by listening to their conversations and correcting if needed. After the groups have had time to meet and discuss, the teacher directs them to get back into the original four groups:

"Wrap up your thoughts. At the count of ten please be back in your groups. One, two, three . . ."

Once the students reconvene in the original groups, they are responsible to share their information with the others and take notes from what the rest of the team has to share. For example, Student 1 from Group 1 is now responsible for sharing his information about conflict with the rest of Group 1. Student 2 from Group 1 is responsible to share her knowledge of rising action with the rest of Group 1.

The jigsaw technique is an easy way to get students involved when a substantial amount of reading is required. Once the activity is over, the teacher can review the essential knowledge to ensure everyone has the key information. The only major drawback of the jigsaw is it takes time. As with any partnering, the teacher should assign the students to groups and make sure the students are arranged with peers who will best advance the learning.

TIPS FOR INCREASING STUDENT ENGAGEMENT IN LECTURES

All educators must lecture. However, research shows the ineffectiveness of relying on lecturing as the primary method of instruction (Ruhl, Hughes, & Schloss, 1987; Bajak, 2014; Chigeza & Halbert, 2014).

A study assessed student learning directly after a lecture to see how much students retained. The results showed that students remembered 70 percent from the first ten minutes. The disappointing news was that the students remembered just 20 percent from the final ten minutes of the lecture (McKeachie, Pintrich, Yi-Guang, & Smith, 1986). Often educators wait until the end of a lecture to deliver the most crucial information.

In 2006, the High School Survey of Student Engagement (HSSSE) was given to over 81,499 students from 26 states. In the survey, two-thirds of the high school students said they were bored in class every day. When asked why, 75 percent stated "the material wasn't interesting to me" and 31 percent said they had "no interaction with the teacher" (Yazzie-Mintz, 2007). A more recent study found only 54 percent of high school students were excited about their classes (National Survey of Student Engagement, 2013). Other research (Penner, 1984) found that the average attention span for a *college student* is between ten and twenty minutes, so imagine what it would be for an average high school student!

Although teachers might like hearing themselves talk, most people, let alone school kids, will begin to cognitively drift away and lose engagement. In order to keep this from happening, there are a variety of active engagement instructional strategies to employ while lecturing (Smith, 2009). When a lecture is the chosen way to deliver content, the teacher should follow these suggestions:

1. Begin the lecture with an interesting question or pose a problem that can be solved using the information that will be provided.
2. Refer to the above questioning strategies throughout the lecture and respond in a positive manner to the answers.
3. Provide written focus questions, lecture notes, a lecture summary, or graphic organizers to the students prior to lecturing.
4. Have students share answers with a partner for questions posed during the lecture.
5. Add joy to the lecture by including humor. Just because something is academic doesn't mean it has to be stone-cold serious.
6. Stay on course and tie in previous student knowledge.
7. Use appropriate tools such as live demonstrations, videos, slide presentations, and other multimedia.
8. Incorporate think/pair/share and let students discuss portions of the lecture in groups to break up the lecture.
9. Keep a brisk pace throughout the lecture.
10. Do not read the lecture to the students. Reading continuously from notes does not allow dialogue and processing time for students to make important connections (Smith, 2009).

Combining the above strategies and tips while lecturing will ultimately lead to livelier lessons and more meaningful learning that students, including those with disabilities, will retain over the long term.

Engagement does not always happen in every classroom. Sixty percent of prospective dropouts affirm lack of value in schoolwork as the main reason for possibly leaving high school (Yazzie-Mintz, 2006). It comes as no surprise that for decades high engagement in learning has consistently been linked to reduced dropout rates and increased levels of student achievement (Blank, 1997; Dary, Pickeral, Shumer, & Williams, 2016). By engaging students, the teacher is also empowering students to learn.

REFLECTION SCENARIO

Mr. Smith, the art teacher at a small charter school, reads over his notes on artist Marc Chagall. He has already posted the objective on the whiteboard the night before—Objective: Review and discuss Marc Chagall.

The students are in for a treat. This is one of his favorite artists and he has so much information that he could talk for hours on the subject. He glances at the clock—10 minutes to go before the students arrive. He turns on the projector, dims the lights, and readies his notes on the lectern.

The bell rings and students arrive. Mr. Smith has only nine students this semester at the high school. The students slide into their seats in the darkened room that has the colorful Marc Chagall print shining on the whiteboard. Mr. Smith takes attendance quickly as students quietly talk with one another. Mr. Smith is up in front of the class welcoming his students and enthusiastically introducing the artist, Marc Chagall. He talks about the context in which Mr. Chagall lived and asks how that affected the content of his art. One student begins to answer, but Mr. Smith goes on.

Mr. Smith progresses through each slide and describes each colorful print as it focuses into view. Students at the back table are quietly doodling. Another student is texting with her phone under the desk. A student in the front row rests her head on the desk, peaking up at the painting. Mr. Smith is gesturing and pointing out the fabulous symbolism in the artist's work. He thinks to himself that he really has the rapt attention of his students today. The students are so engaged in the art of Marc Chagall.

Are the students engaged and how do you know? What is the evidence? In what ways might you change Mr. Smith's lesson to ensure engagement and be able to check for understanding?

Chapter 9

Multiple Intelligences and a Growth Mindset

It has been my observation that the happiest of people, the vibrant doers of the world, are almost always those who are using—who are putting into play, calling upon, depending upon—the greatest number of their God-given talents and capabilities.

—John Glenn

Knowledge speaks, but wisdom listens.

—Jimi Hendrix

Developmental psychologist Howard Gardner changed approaches to teaching and learning in the 1980s with his Theory of Multiple Intelligences. Gardner defines intelligence as "the capacity to solve problems or to fashion products that are valued in one or more cultural settings" (Gardner & Hatch, 1989). In other cultural settings, settings outside of school, forms of intelligence are valued that are not valued in school, according to Gardner's research. Schools tend to focus on verbal-linguistic (the ability to read, write, and speak) and mathematical-logical (the ability to work with numbers) intelligences, but other types of intelligence are not used to teach or to demonstrate learning.

Each person has a unique intellectual profile that is made up of a combination of intelligences. Most people have all of the intelligences to some degree, but they have preferences and strengths. Through biology and experience, individuals develop some intelligences more than others and become stronger in certain areas.

Gardner's research led him to identify what are now eight types of intelligence (originally there were seven, but the eighth was added after his research was initially published).

1. *Verbal-linguistic*: This intelligence is characterized by the ability to use spoken and written language, as seen in poets, teachers, and lawyers.
2. *Mathematical-logical.* This intelligence is associated with scientific investigation, mathematical calculations, and logical thinking, as seen in accountants, scientists, or computer programmers.
3. *Musical.* This intelligence encompasses the ability to discern and appreciate musical patterns. These learners have an affinity for reproducing/manipulating sound, creating their own melodies, or improvising over another piece of music. Musicians and composers, not surprisingly, have this strength.
4. *Visual-spatial.* This intelligence is characterized by the ability to think visually and the capacity for abstract thinking. The person who can quickly find the most efficient way to pack a large number of oddly shaped belongings into the back of a car has spatial intelligence. Artists, structural engineers, and designers would have this strength.
5. *Bodily-kinesthetic.* This intelligence is characterized by physical coordination and a preference for bodily movement. Athletes and dancers would fall into this category.
6. *Interpersonal.* This intelligence is characterized by the ability to understand and react to other people's needs, desires, and motivations. Interpersonal intelligence enables people to work well with others, such as psychologists, counselors, teachers, and sales people.
7. *Intrapersonal.* This intelligence is characterized by self-awareness and an understanding of one's own thoughts and feelings. These students tend to be introspective. Poets, psychologists, or philosophers would be examples of people with high intrapersonal intelligence.
8. *Naturalist.* This intelligence is characterized by an ability to care for nature and to connect with the outdoors. These students understand the cycle of life. Biologists, forestry professionals, or river guides would have naturalist intelligence.

HAVING A GROWTH MINDSET

While the benefits of Gardner's Theory of Multiple Intelligences include increased attention to meeting students' individual needs and varying learning activities and forms of assessment to accommodate different learning styles, there are some criticisms of the way that multiple intelligences have been used to make assumptions about learners (and to cause learners to make assumptions about themselves). Although a student might favor a certain type of intelligence or learning style, there is empirical evidence of neuroplasticity, or brain plasticity, which means intelligence is not fixed but can be grown (Boaler, 2013). When the brain is learning something new, the internal structure of the neurons change, increasing the number of synapses (Drubach, 2000). The brain has the ability to change and grow, and the environment the teacher creates in the classroom can either help or hinder this growth.

Researcher and author Carol Dweck contends that students' mindset, what they believe they are capable of achieving, plays a huge role in their motivation and achievement. According to Dweck, the teacher's effort to help students develop a *growth mindset* (a belief that intelligence can be grown) rather than a *fixed mindset* (the belief that either you have a strength or you don't, and that's just the way it is) has proven to produce huge academic gains (Dweck, 2015). When students and teachers have a growth mindset, student achievement flourishes.

In light of this research, the problem with identifying students' types of intelligence and continually teaching to and assessing according to those intelligences is that it teaches and reinforces a fixed rather than a growth mindset. Areas of "weakness" should not be avoided because the student might, at first, "get it wrong." When students make an error or struggle with learning content, and they have to think about why something is wrong or hard to understand, new synaptic connects are made and the mind grows (Boaler, 2013). Dweck maintains, "It is about telling the truth about a student's current achievement and then, together, doing something about it, helping him or her become smarter" (Dweck, 2015). Mistakes are good learning tools as long as teachers help the students learn from mistakes and do not just praise their effort.

Multiple studies conducted in different parts of the world (England, Israel, and the United States), all came to the same conclusion: Ability grouping produces lower achievement than mixed-ability grouping (Linchevski & Kutscher, 1998; Dweck, 2006; Blatchford, Hallam, Kutnick, & Creech, 2008; Alexander, 2010; Boaler, 2013). This is not to be confused with flexibly grouping students briefly to reteach or enrich content based on formal assessment data. Briefly grouping students to work on a specific skill has been found to be an effective intervention for all students, including those with disabilities (Tkatchov & DeVries, 2017).

USING MULTIPLE INTELLIGENCES APPROPRIATELY

As long as the teacher encourages all students to grow and does not make excuses for students who "just are not good" at something, they can use knowledge of the multiple intelligences to create enriching learning activities and assessment opportunities. Here are some tips for incorporating the multiple intelligences into instruction:

1. Do not feel the need to incorporate all eight of the intelligences into one lesson.
2. Try to incorporate activities throughout the lesson that provide an arena for more than one intelligence to shine at a time (Williams, Blythe, White, Sternberg, & Gardner, 1996).
3. Make sure to hold all students accountable for the activity, even if the activity is not built around an intelligence that is their strength. To say that an athletic student does not need to complete an assignment because it does not contain any bodily-kinesthetic outlet would be unrealistic and counterproductive.
4. For assessments, provide options that target different learning styles but still assess the same learning goal.
5. Keep track of which intelligences have been included in learning activities. If one intelligence is not being implemented regularly, take note and address that intelligence in an upcoming lesson or activity.

In many cases these intelligences will overlap, and for most students they do. These multiple intelligences are not independent of themselves and usually correlate with at least four others (McGreal, 2013). For example, most good writers will show strong verbal-linguistic strengths as well as intrapersonal skills. Most mathematically savvy students will excel in both logical and spatial activities. Teachers can provide questionnaires to students regarding their learning strengths (there are tons of these to be found on the Internet) or in time, as they get to know their class, the different learning strengths of the students naturally appear.

ADAPTING YOUR CLASSROOM INSTRUCTION FOR VISUAL, AUDITORY, KINESTHETIC, AND TACTILE LEARNERS

Research shows that the majority of students use their senses in the learning process in four modalities: visual, auditory, kinesthetic, and tactile. As with the multiple intelligences, learners tend to have preferences in learning modalities. In a general education classroom (Reiff, 1992; Stronck, 1980; Eislzer, 1983; Meier, 2000), preferences in learning modalities might break down in these numbers:

- 25–30 percent visual learners
- 25–30 percent auditory learners

- 15 percent tactile/kinesthetic learners
- 25–30 percent mixed modalities (usually a mixture of visual combined with one of the other three modalities)

Therefore, only 30 percent of the students may remember most of what is said in a classroom lecture, and only 30 percent may remember what is primarily seen.

The following are suggestions for enhancing classroom instruction for each of the four learning modalities to increase the likelihood that all students will learn.

Visual learners can better recall what they have observed or read. They benefit from images, graphs, diagrams, and illustrations. They want to know what the subject looks like. Teachers can best communicate to them by providing handouts, diagrams, mind maps, bulleted lists, word webs, videos, visuals, and other forms of graphic organizers. While reading, visual learners could use highlighters to mark important words or information. To best serve visual learners, try not to give only oral instructions without accompanying written instructions.

Products for the visual modality:

- Dioramas
- Drawings
- Flow charts
- Storyboards
- Plays
- Maps
- Designs
- Collages
- Paintings
- Slide shows
- Bulletin boards
- Web pages
- Pamphlets
- Cartoon strips
- Photo journals
- Data tables
- Graphs
- Banners
- Mobiles
- Storyboard

Auditory learners learn best by listening as well as talking. They are good at remembering things that they hear. They often read to themselves as they study. They are also often distracted by noise and sounds. Auditory learners tend to be good storytellers. Auditory learners are more likely to remember lectures, especially when accompanied by discussion; in fact, discussing what they read and hear helps them to remember it. Teachers can best communicate with them by speaking clearly and asking questions. Verbal repetition is a helpful means of studying for auditory learners.

Teachers should provide oral instructions for assignments, even if the instructions are provided in writing. Include whole group and partner discussions in your class when appropriate (Deci, Vallerand, Pelletier, & Ryan, 1991). Provide students with videos or audio recordings to complement written text. Allow time for students to read out loud or talk when problem solving. Provide breaks from silent reading periods. Tools to use when teaching include read-alouds, debates, discussions, interviews, lectures, audio books, plays, radio/podcasts, and songs.

Products for the auditory modality:

- Plays
- Debates
- Dialogues
- Newscasts
- Podcasts
- Commercials
- Speeches
- Acting
- Interviews
- Story reading
- Skits
- Oral reports
- Song

Kinesthetic learners learn through movement and action. They need to experience what they are learning. They process information best from hands-on, team activities that include changing seats and moving around (Jones, 2007). They remember best by writing or physically manipulating the information (Meier, 2000). These learners generally do not like lecture or discussion classes, but prefer to actually "do something."

Kinesthetic learners, when they must sit, benefit from sitting at the front of the class to help them to stay focused. Some kinesthetic learners seem fidgety; they have a hard time sitting still in class. Many kids who are diagnosed with attention deficit disorder (ADD) or attention deficit hyperactivity disorder (ADHD) are kinesthetic learners.

Products for the bodily-kinesthetic modality:

- Dance
- Games
- Role plays
- Skits
- Exercise routines
- Demonstrations

Tactile learners learn through touching and feeling. They prefer "hands-on" activities and appreciate when manipulatives are included in the learning (Powell, 2013). Textures and 3D models can accentuate the learning for these students.

Products for the tactile modality:

- Puzzles
- Clay models
- Tracing
- Sand trays
- Replicas
- Textured posters
- Building a machine

To engage all learners, teachers should vary instruction not only from day to day but also within a single class period and provide students with many opportunities to complete hands-on work.

REFLECTION SCENARIO

Ms. Bewley teaches a poetry unit each year. She has students write poems and recite them for their classmates in a variety of ways. Students can choose to act out poems, weave poetry into original songs played with guitars, or present videos they created reading their poetry in the background. This year, she asked students to present at a coffee shop to enhance student engagement. Reflect on units that you have taught in the past. In what ways might you give students opportunities that involve multiple intelligences? Also, in what ways could you promote a growth mindset and encourage students to develop in areas that are not their strengths?

Chapter 10

Accessing Background Knowledge to Assist Learning

Before you can really start setting financial goals, you need to determine where you stand financially.

—David Bach

Students are continually faced with new information. How do they make sense of this information and, more importantly, connect the new learning to their understanding of the world? The National Research Council identified three key findings about how new learning takes place based on studies in human development, neuroscience, and psychology (National Research Council, 1999):

- "A metacognitive approach to instruction can help students learn to take control of their own learning by defining learning goals and monitoring their progress in achieving them."
- "Students come to the classroom with preconceptions about how the world works. If their initial understanding is not engaged, they may fail to grasp the new concepts and information that are taught, or they may learn them for purposes of a test but revert to their preconceptions outside the classroom."
- "To develop competence in an area of inquiry, students must: (a) have a deep foundation of factual knowledge, (b) understand facts and ideas in the context of a conceptual framework, and (c) organize knowledge in ways that facilitate retrieval and application."

These findings rely on *background knowledge* to make sense of new information, categorize it, and make connections to items already known. Without background knowledge, these three key areas that need to be in place for people to learn are in jeopardy.

One way to apply the National Reach Council's findings about the importance of prior knowledge in classroom practice is to incorporate wait time, which gives the students time to recall information. As mentioned in previous chapters, *wait time* refers to the time given for students to recall information. In the field of education there are basically three types of wait time (Lipton, Wellman, & Humbard, 2001):

1. *The amount of time the teacher pauses after asking a question.* Based on the complexity of the question, this time can range from two seconds for an easy question to five or six seconds for a complex question. This time allows the student the opportunity to actually think.
2. *The amount of time the teacher pauses after providing a response.* This time allows students to make sense of the response and organize it with their previous knowledge of the topic.
3. *The amount of time a teacher pauses before responding to a comment or question.* This pause shows that the teacher is thinking about his/her thinking (metacognition) and modeling good practice. It is a gesture to show the question deserves a well-thought-out answer.

This seems simple, but sometimes it is difficult for a teacher to wait five seconds after asking a question. Waiting before jumping in with an answer can be difficult. Effective teachers make sure to consciously wait after asking questions or answering complex questions so the student has time to process the information.

Another way to implement the National Research Council's findings is through *inquiry*. The term "inquiry" refers to the exploration of knowledge by asking questions about what is already known and what one believes he/she will learn. By using inquiry, students can better organize the information they know or are learning. This organization allows students to apply what was learned in new situation and connect it to previous background knowledge (National Research Panel, 1999).

Background knowledge is acquired through our ability to process and store information and the number of experiences that directly tie to our knowledge of content encountered in school (Marzano, 2004). Students lacking ample background knowledge, or those who cannot activate prior knowledge possibly due to a disability, may struggle to contribute and achieve throughout the curriculum, no matter how much wait time a teacher provides. In these cases, the teacher must explicitly provide background knowledge or build in items like graphic organizers to assist in the retrieval of previous knowledge. This is especially true when reading is involved; a strong correlation is found between prior knowledge and reading comprehension (Langer, 1984; Guthrie, 2008). Dr. Anita Archer, one of the foremost experts in reading instruction today, considers vocabulary and background knowledge two of the "building blocks of reading instruction" (Archer & Hughes, 2011).

Use these strategies to increase student background knowledge:

- Spend a little time before lessons begin to assist students in making connections to prior lessons and past learning. Before teaching a new concept or unit, it is important that the teacher find out what students already know about the topic, therefore providing the teacher with data about what background knowledge the class currently has (Lent, 2012).
- Include activities that reflect the cultural diversity of the classroom and support multiple intelligences.
- Use graphic organizers as a tool to help students trigger prior knowledge and categorize new information.
- Engage students in meaningful activities that incorporate prior learning.
- Let students experiment; allow them to test their preconceptions or confirm what they believe to be true.
- Use cooperative grouping to share prior knowledge between students.
- Involve community members as educational peers and create "mentoring relationships." This will create tutors with residential and cultural similarities to specific student populations (Marzano, 2004).
- Use video to provide students with images of other countries and past events. When taken in small, collaborative groups guided by the teacher, these "virtual field trips" can build background knowledge, engage students in academic dialogue, advance higher-order thinking skills, and increase vocabulary development (Mandel, 1999; Sriarunrasmee, Praweenya, & Dachakupt, 2015).
- Constantly evaluate instruction to ensure it builds on what students know.

As addressed deeper in chapter 11, effective teachers utilize background knowledge to teach vocabulary in the following ways:

- Beginning with student-friendly information about the word's meaning.
- Prompting students to use the word.
- Bringing the word back in a variety of formal and informal ways.
- Getting students to take the word learning beyond the classroom.
- Helping students use context productively (Beck, McKeown, & Kucan, 2003).
- Utilizing pre-reading activities, such as discussing the content of a story, linking a common experience, and explaining problematic items relevant to the reading materials (Droop & Verhoeven, 2003).

The importance of background knowledge is not new. Researchers William Christen and Thomas Murphy proclaimed more than 25 years ago, "It appears that providing students with strategies to activate their prior knowledge base or to build a base if one does not exist is supported by the current research. It is our contention that this is one way teachers can have a positive influence on comprehension in their classrooms" (Christen & Murphy, 1991).

In conclusion, students must construct new understanding of material, create paradigm shifts, and deconstruct prior misunderstandings to effectively learn. The ability to perform these tasks is essential to learning because background knowledge is used to make sense of new information as well as helps categorize and make connections of what is being learned. Students lacking adequate background knowledge will struggle to access, contribute, and advance throughout the curriculum.

REFLECTION SCENARIO

A fifth-grade teacher in a rural classroom in Hawaii introduced the book about Balto, the sled dog who was instrumental in getting a diphtheria antitoxin from Anchorage to Nenana, Alaska, to prevent an outbreak of the disease. The Iditarod is the sled dog race on the Iditarod Trail in Alaska that is run each year to commemorate the feat. Many children at this school had never even been outside of their Hawaiian village, so they had no experience with snow or dog sled races. How might the teacher shore up the students' lack of background knowledge to make the reading of the story of Balto more meaningful?

Chapter 11

Reading Instruction for All Teachers

When I approach a child, he inspires in me two sentiments: tenderness for what he is, and respect for what he may become.

—Louis Pasteur

The aim of education must be the training of independently acting and thinking individuals who can see in the service to the community their highest life achievement.

—Albert Einstein

I do it, we do it, you do it.

—Anita Archer

There is a direct correlation between poverty and illiteracy. Per the Literacy Project Foundation, three out of four people on welfare cannot read. Fifty percent of unemployed individuals between 16 and 21 years of age are not considered literate. On the flip side, as the literacy rate doubles, so does the per capita income.

Based on findings from a 1995 study, an average preschool child from a professional family was provided experiences with eleven million words per year, a working-class family six million words, and a family living in poverty three million words (Hart & Risley, 1995). A more recent study (Reardon & Portilla, 2016) has shown this gap to have closed by around 10 percent, but the difference of preschooler word knowledge based on parent income is still unacceptable.

Vocabulary attainment in early grades is a significant predictor of reading comprehension ten years later (Cunningham & Stanovich, 1997; Phillips, Gormley, & Anderson, 2016). Students with limited vocabulary in the third grade have diminished comprehension scores at the end of elementary school (Chall, Jacobs, & Baldwin, 1990). The more vocabulary a child possesses early in life, the higher the chance of academic success later in life.

It is the role of every teacher, not just the English teacher, to effectively teach vocabulary. Vocabulary, like background knowledge, is needed to truly comprehend a topic or skill. Many content areas, especially mathematics, social studies, and science, have deep reading components that depend on understanding content-specific vocabulary (Gaston, Martinez, & Martin, 2016). For example, to truly master mathematics, students must not only know symbolic notation, graphs, and visual displays, but also must understand how mathematical terms like *volume* and *angle* are similar or different when used in a mathematics setting compared to other content areas (Meiers & Trevitt, 2010). Because new words come up in all subject areas, no matter the grade or the subject, it is necessary that all teachers know how to explicitly and effectively teach vocabulary.

Researchers postulate that *explicit instruction* in vocabulary achieves positive results for diverse populations of students, including those with disabilities (Rosenshine, 1986; Archer, 2007). Explicit instruction means structured and systematic teaching that uses an effective methodology (Archer & Hughes, 2010).

Unfortunately, research shows that explicit vocabulary instruction is not a daily practice in many classrooms (Dunn, Bonner, & Huske, 2007; Herzfeldt-Kamprath & Ullrich, 2016). For example, a teacher who puts up a word wall but does not directly teach those words is *not* explicitly helping the learner master new vocabulary. Asking students to find the definitions of words in a dictionary is also, on its own, ineffective. Studies have shown that around 60 percent of students incorrectly use a word if only a dictionary definition is given (Hatzivassiloglou & McKeown, 1993).

Anita Archer and other researchers suggest explicitly teaching words that are necessary to understand the concept, but more importantly words that the students will see again, connecting to real-world application versus simply the academic setting. As a member of a school team, grade-level team, or individually, educators can create a list of important words to teach or utilize predetermined word lists like the Coxhead Academic Word List.

For explicitly teaching a single vocabulary word, teachers should first provide a description and an example of the new term. Next, the students restate the description or example in *their own words*. This is important as they attach their own background knowledge to the new term. Finally, the teacher creates opportunities for the students and himself/herself to use the word in conversation or within lessons. Repeatedly saying and using a word allows students to have a better grasp of the term and store it into memory (Fay & Cutler, 1977).

Students can also represent the new words in linguistic and nonlinguistic forms. One way to represent a word in a nonlinguistic form is by using *visual imagery*, or a visual representation (a picture or drawing) of the word. Studies have shown that students who used imagery when learning vocabulary performed 37 percentile points higher than students who were just asked to continuously repeat the definition and 21 percentile points higher than students who used the new words only in complete sentences (Marzano & Pickering, 2005). Visual imagery can also assist students in strengthening relationships between words and noticing small differences in word meaning (Huey & Swinehart, 2015). Having students draw a picture of a word might seem silly, especially in the upper grades, but it is an effective technique to add to vocabulary instruction.

VOCABULARY WHILE READING

There are multiple opportunities within a lesson when vocabulary instruction can occur. Dr. Archer offers these examples of how to teach vocabulary during three different times within a lesson. These examples are applicable to all content areas.

Before Reading a Passage

The teacher should introduce the pronunciation of words that are important to the passage and provide simple examples of meaning for these words. As stated before, these words should be important to the content and ideally words that students will see again, even in other subjects. The teacher then provides engaging instruction on selected vocabulary.

This engaging instruction can include using items like word maps, critical attribute templates, word diagrams, as well as other templates (sample templates are provided at the end of the chapter). These templates can also be used to scaffold learning for struggling students.

During this time, the teacher can teach or activate background knowledge. What do the students already know about the subject or this word? The teacher can tie in previously known information that is relevant to the new vocabulary.

Next, the teacher assists the students in previewing the chapter. Previewing can be done by having the students read the headings and subheadings and ensuring the students understand the words used in the headings and subheadings. The teacher can pose questions like, "As you preview the chapter, how do you see the new vocabulary as being relevant? What connections do you see?" This can assist the students in understanding the information that will be covered and establishing a purpose for reading.

The teacher can also introduce strategies that students can utilize during reading, such as note-taking skills, graphic organizers, and word or concept mapping.

During Reading a Passage

The teacher and students can generate questions while reading the material. Generating questions about the passage helps students remain attentive while reading and self-check if it is being understood or if any vocabulary words are unknown (Palincsar, Brown, & Campione, 1993). Studies have shown that by increasing the rigor of comprehension questions, students will learn more and have a deeper understanding of content (Langer, 2001; Francis, 2016).

The teacher can provide a study guide for students to use. The study guide can include vocabulary for students to keep track of and help students understand where they are supposed to be and what they are supposed to learn.

After Passage Reading

After reading the passage, the teacher assists the students in using or creating a graphic organizer to summarize the information they just read. Summarizing is a great skill that helps students retain important information and reflect on vocabulary learned in the reading.

As mentioned earlier in the chapter, the teacher must continue to provide opportunities for students to practice using new vocabulary terms. The more times the students use the words, the more chances the teacher has to correct the usage and the more times the students have to master the new term.

Studies on the characteristics of effective vocabulary instruction (Marzano & Pickering, 2005) confirm this approach to teaching new words:

1. Effective vocabulary instruction does not rely solely on dictionary definitions.
2. Students must represent their knowledge of words in linguistic and nonlinguistic ways.

3. Effective vocabulary instruction involves the gradual shaping of word meanings through multiple exposures.
4. Teaching word parts enhances students' understanding of terms.
5. Different types of words require different types of instruction.
6. Students should discuss the terms they are learning.
7. Students should play with words.
8. Instruction should focus on terms that have a high probability of enhancing academic success.

NONREADERS

Evidence shows that after the early elementary grades, children's interest in reading sharply declines (McKenna, Kear, & Ellsworth, 1995). One reason is as the reading level increases in difficulty, students need to work harder and utilize strategies to figure out meaning or to gain understanding. Unfortunately, many struggling readers have not mastered these strategies for successful reading. By effectively teaching vocabulary before, during, and after reading a passage, teachers can limit the number of students who will become disinterested and unmotivated to read.

A teacher's first instinct to assist students who are struggling with vocabulary might be to simplify the assignment or limit the number of words the student needs to read. This is one of the worst things a teacher can do. Limiting the vocabulary of a struggling student causes the student to get further behind while advanced students get further ahead. This is called "the Matthew Effect," meaning that "the rich get richer and the poor get poorer" (Archer, 2007). Good readers read more and grow vocabulary as poor readers read less and remain limited in vocabulary. Effective teachers provide instruction and the same vocabulary to all students, as well as provide scaffolding to those who need a little more assistance, time, or support.

For students who continue to be disinterested and unmotivated to read even after they have shown understanding of the vocabulary, research recommends that teachers try the following strategies (Guthrie & Humenick, 2004):

1. Build student independence by allowing choices of texts and assignments.
2. Produce opportunities for students' social interactions to be focused on learning and understanding from text.
3. Ensure a variety of interesting texts are accessible to students.
4. Focus students on significant and interesting learning goals.

If there is one item that gives students the best shot at productive post-school lives, it is to leave school being functionally literate and understanding the opportunities that reading can unleash.

REFLECTION SCENARIO

You peek your head into your next-door teacher's classroom to see if she has a working set of dry-erase markers, as yours stopped working during a classroom activity. She is in the middle of a vocabulary lesson. You hear her say the next word is "countenance."

"Who knows what countenance means? Rachel?"

Rachel says, "Doesn't it mean counting in a certain way?"

The teacher replies, "No, that's not quite it. Does anyone else have an idea what countenance means?"

Juan's hand goes up. The teacher calls on Juan and he offers, "I think it means some kind of emotion."

The teacher responds, "You're getting closer."

This drags on another minute as individual students give unsatisfactory answers. The teacher finally asks someone to look up the word in the dictionary.

Many experts refer to this as a "fishing expedition" and caution that students will retain the first, often incorrect, meaning offered. Many of us are guilty of using this method one time or another. In what ways do you see this as being detrimental to the vocabulary process and instruction? Apply some of the strategies mentioned in this chapter to rewrite the scenario. How would explicit vocabulary instruction look in this classroom?

VOCABULARY WORD TEMPLATES

A *word map* (Schwartz, 1988; Schwartz & Raphael, 1985) is exactly what it sounds like: a map that helps fit the word into prior knowledge to create a context for the word that makes sense. A word map usually has the vocabulary word in the middle of the template, a user-friendly definition, three items that are similar to the word, and three examples of the word (see Figure 11.1).

For example, if the word was "large," a user-friendly definition could be "greater than average in size." Three items similar could be huge, big, and gigantic. Three examples could include an elephant, a skyscraper, and a father's pant size. The student needs to create these examples so the vocabulary word makes sense and connects to their prior knowledge.

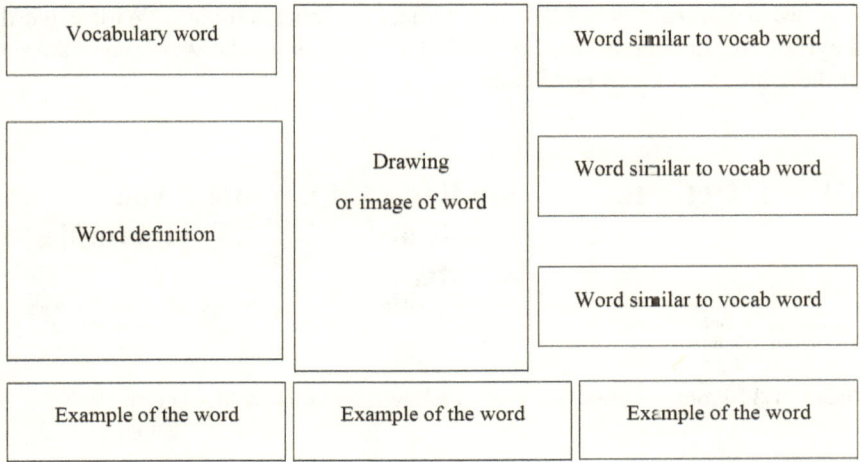

Figure 11.1 Word Map. Adapted from Frayer, Frederick, & Klausmeier, 1969.

A *critical attribute template* is another device that can be used to teach vocabulary. With a critical attribute template, the student writes down the vocabulary word as well as the part of speech to which the word belongs. Next, the student lists three to five critical attributes that define the vocabulary word. Finally, the student either writes the word in a sentence, draws an illustration, or provides examples of the word in the final column.

Word and Part of Speech	Critical Attributes or Features	Sentence/Illustration/Examples
Texas noun	• Second largest state • Located in south central United States	*(outline drawing of Texas)*

Figure 11.2 Critical Attribute Template. Adapted from Frayer, Frederick, & Klausmeier, 1969.

A *word diagram* is similar to a critical attribute template. With a word diagram, the student writes the word, the definition of the word, an example of the word, and then a nonexample.

Word	Definition	Similar words or actions	Example	Non-Example
Implement	To put something into effect, or to carry something out	Starting something	Putting a plan into action	Just thinking about doing something

Figure 11.3 Word Diagram. Adapted from Frayer, Frederick, & Klausmeier, 1969.

This template can assist students in organizing the similarities and differences between items.

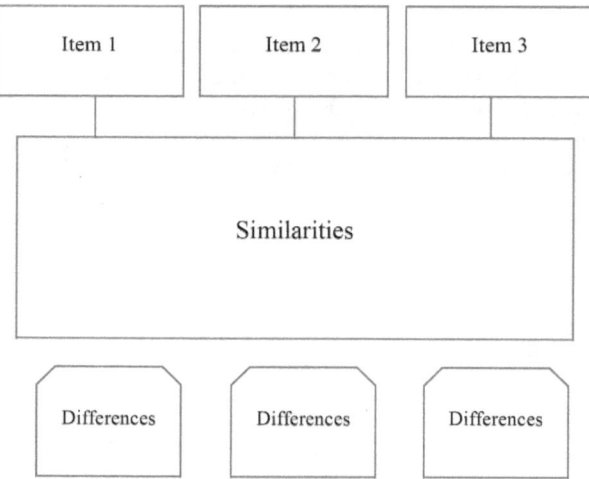

Figure 11.4 Similarities and Differences Template. Adapted from Frayer, Frederick, & Klausmeier, 1969.

Chapter 12

Writing Instruction for All Teachers

I prefer tongue-tied knowledge to ignorant loquacity.

—Marcus Tullius Cicero

We don't know all the answers. If we knew all the answers we'd be bored, wouldn't we? We keep looking, searching, trying to get more knowledge.

—Jack LaLanne

Just as the authors of this book believe that every teacher is responsible for vocabulary instruction, they also believe that every teacher is responsible for writing instruction. It is hard to find a class in which a student isn't writing something, and if a student is writing, it is the job of the educator to help the student be successful. Humans need a means of communication, and when the opportunity to communicate through using spoken words or visual signs is not an option, writing becomes a way to build on or extend the range of that communication (Kucer, 2009).

The most groundbreaking research on what elements should be included in writing instruction comes from the publication *Writing Next: Effective Strategies to Improve Writing of Adolescents in Middle and High Schools* (Graham & Perin, 2007). This publication provided elements found in effective writing instruction, and although it is geared toward middle school and high school, the elements can be adapted for earlier grades as well.

Writing Next identified 11 elements of writing instruction found to be effective for helping students learn to write and use writing as a tool for their learning. This book will focus on eight of the elements: *writing strategies, summarization, collaborative writing, specific product goals, sentence combining, prewriting, study of models,* and *writing for content learning.* As stated in chapter 13 of this book, assessment data should be taken into account to specify which element is best suited for a specific class or student. There is not enough time in the school year to randomly try forms of instruction and hope that they will work.

WRITING STRATEGIES

It is crucial that educators teach students strategies for preparing, revising, and editing their work. Various studies have shown that the quality of student work increases when teachers previously covered ways to plan, revise, and edit compositions (Bonk & Graham, 2006). Brainstorming, outlining, paragraph shrinking, and peer revising are forms of writing strategies.

One way to teach writing strategies is through the *self-regulated strategy development* (SRSD) approach. This approach has been found to be effective with all students, including those with disabilities (Graham & Perin, 2007; Englert, 2009; Reid, Lienemann, & Hagaman, 2013). This metacognitive approach assists students in thinking about their writing and self-regulating their effort. Good writers understand the writing process; they understand the need for preparing, monitoring, evaluating, and revising (Hamlin, 2011). SRSD is an approach to writing that explicitly walks struggling writers through this process in six stages:

- *Develop background knowledge.* The teacher and the student examine the criteria for good writing. What does the student already know about effective writing?
- Example: *"Marissa, what do you currently do when trying to organize ideas for a paper?"*
- *Discuss strategies.* The teacher and student discuss the student's current writing performance as well as strategies he/she currently uses. The teacher shares a new strategy or strategies the student might try to apply and explains the benefit of committing to the new strategy.
- Example: *"Clustering is a great strategy to use. With clustering, you chose one word, a nucleus word, and write it down. Then we start to think of things connected to the word. If some topics seem connected, we will circle them and 'cluster' that idea."*
- *Model the strategy.* The teacher models the strategy for the student, thinking aloud so the student is able to hear what the teacher is thinking while applying the strategy.
- Example: *"Let's practice this. If we picked the word 'bullying,' what other thoughts or words come to mind? Let's write the word 'bullying' on the*

paper, and then write each new thought we have. Hmmm, I think of aggressive behavior. I guess that can happen verbally, or socially, or even physically. Maybe I will circle those three together—it looks like I can cluster them together as types *of bullying."*
- *Memorize the strategies.* Student memorizes the steps of the new strategy.
- Example: *"So if the clustering strategy consists of picking a keyword, thinking about that word and clustering ideas together until we have enough ideas for the paper, then finally writing a few sentences for each cluster, what's a way we can remember that strategy? What if we tried to remember the terms 'word-cluster-write', or WCW?"*
- *Support the student in the strategies.* The teacher continues to provide assistance as the student applies the new strategy to writing assignments.
- Example: *"Marissa, I see you have a key term for this paper. What is the next step in the cluster strategy we used last time?"*
- *Allow independent practice.* The student is able to apply the strategy to future writing assignments without any teacher assistance or support.

Because SRSD does not have to be administered linearly, teachers can reorganize, adjust, and jump around the six steps based on student need (Painter, 2016).

SUMMARIZATION

Summarization entails teaching students a system of how to summarize texts or concisely restate the main ideas in their own words. One example is the use of an index card. A well-written summary should be able to fit in that 3 × 5 space. Summarization helps students retain information.

COLLABORATIVE WRITING

Collaborative writing allows students to work in teams to plan, outline, revise, and edit their compositions. When pairing students, do not let "birds of a feather flock together" by placing the lowest scoring students together (Smith, 2009). It is also imperative that the highest scoring student is not placed with the lowest scoring student. Use this system: If you have 30 kids in the class, rank them by ability. Place student 1 with student 15, 2 with 16, and so on.

Once the partnerships are formed, tell the students to work as partners on a specific writing task. Throughout the task, monitor the classroom and assist as necessary while providing specific feedback.

SPECIFIC PRODUCT GOALS

Specific product goals provide students with objectives to focus on particular aspects of their writing. In other words, the teacher assigns students specific, reachable goals for the writing they are to complete. This could focus on a specific writing trait, such as developing a controlling ideas or theme, applying smooth transitions, using appropriate voice, or utilizing effective word choice.

SENTENCE COMBINING

Sentence-combining instruction involves teaching students to construct more complex and sophisticated sentences by combining two or more basic sentences. Sentence combining is an effective way for students to improve their syntax (the way words are put together in sentences). Sentence combining should allow students to play with writing as they explore different ways to put sentences together (Dean, 2008).

An easy way of teaching sentence combining is to give students short sentences, called kernel sentences, and then have them chunk the information together into one effective sentence (Strong, 1986). For example:

The girl danced around.
The girl was four years old.
The girl was named Madeline.
Combined sentence: The four-year-old girl named Madeline danced around.

Sentence combining can be utilized for most students, including those with disabilities, in an inclusive, a self-contained, or a resource room setting (Saddler & Asaro-Saddler, 2010). For example, it can be a great hands-on activity using cut outs of words that can be moved around.

PREWRITING

Prewriting, like writing strategies, helps students organize their work—in this case before they even start the assignment. Prewriting can include gathering possible information, making a visual representation, group planning, or reading materials and taking notes on the topic they will begin to write about. Providing the opportunity to plan prior to writing has been proven to improve writing quality (Lorenz, Green, & Brown, 2009). The simple act of providing time and instruction on how to prewrite can be extremely beneficial to struggling writers. The use of a graphic organizer, as discussed in previous chapters, can provide a beneficial structure for these types of prewriting activities (Keeler, 2013).

STUDY OF MODELS

Study of models provides students with opportunities to read and analyze good writing. This will also provide the students with an exemplar of what the teacher is looking for in a good paper. When using models, the teacher should explain to students the critical elements, patterns, and forms that create the exemplary piece. When studying models, provide examples of exemplary writing and explain exactly why the writing samples are exemplars. Also show examples of poor writing and explain what is missing in these samples as well as what would be needed to make these samples exemplary.

WRITING FOR CONTENT LEARNING

Writing for content learning involves students writing in every class, no matter what. An individual teacher might not have much control in this, but can educate peers as to why writing in every class is important. The more a student writes with specific feedback from the teacher, the higher the quality will become.

REFLECTION SCENARIO

Your students' writing scores are low and your team meets to consider strategies to implement school-wide that will help students to organize thoughts and practice summarizing skills. What are some strategies that you might suggest to your colleagues? How would you implement these strategies in your classroom? How can you tailor them to your content area?

Chapter 13

Assessing *for* Learning and Assessment *of* Learning

Did They Learn It, and What Evidence Do You Have?

> Without question . . . students must be regarded as the most important users of classroom assessment results.
>
> —Richard J. Stiggins

Margaret Heritage, considered one of the most prominent experts in assessment, uses the analogy of a patient's visit to the doctor to describe assessment. The doctor gathers data by asking probing questions of the patient, and the patient gives the doctor feedback in the responses and the results of the examination. The doctor is assessing the situation to figure out the best course of treatment to improve the patient's health.

An educator in his/her profession is very much like a doctor when using assessment for teacher and student to understand what is needed to improve the student's learning. The doctor does not rely on one test to diagnose the patient and will not give all patients the same tests. Tests will depend on the individual patient's circumstances. Assessing for learning (AfL) is like a check up at a doctor's office.

OVERVIEW OF ASSESSMENT

AfL is truly a part of the minute-to-minute, day-to-day teaching and learning in the classroom. Some type of assessment needs to take place for a teacher to really know if a student has learned information. Assessment provides evidence regarding the extent to which the student understands a concept as well as how well the teacher taught the concept and what instructional adjustments the teacher might need to make to accommodate the varying needs of students.

Simply put, researcher Rick Stiggins (2017) defines assessment as "the process of gathering information to inform education-related decisions." Since a teacher's job is to assist students in obtaining new knowledge and skills and in becoming lifelong learners, regularly assessing each student's learning is an essential aspect of teaching. Assessment allows the teacher to collect data to verify that the students are learning essential knowledge and skills.

Examples of Knowledge (what students should know):

- Vocabulary
- Terminology
- Definitions
- Facts
- Locations
- Details
- Events/people
- Timeline

Examples of Skills (what students should be able to do):

- Decode
- Computate
- Listen
- Speak
- Write
- Compare
- Infer
- Analyze
- Interpret
- Inquire
- Investigate
- Problem-solve
- Note take/outline
- Work with group

A teacher cannot know if a student has obtained new knowledge or skills without AfL and assessment *of* learning. Assessment can occur in multiple ways: in the beginning of a lesson to see what the students already know (diagnostic assessment), informally throughout the lesson (the formative assessment process), or at the end of learning (summative assessment). The alignment of these different occurrences in assessment is called a *balanced assessment system.*

BALANCED ASSESSMENT SYSTEM

Different types of assessments have different purposes and can happen at different times with different frequencies. This is called a balanced assessment

Assessing for *Learning and Assessment* of *Learning* 93

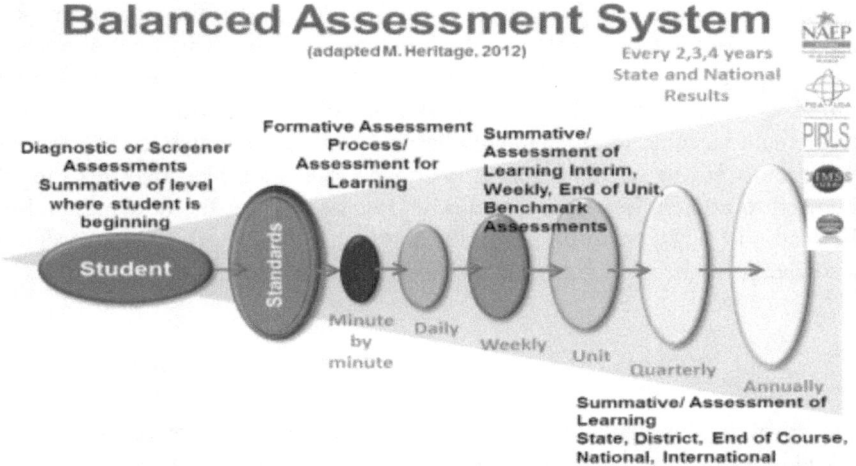

Figure 13.1 Balanced Assessment System From Heritage, M. (2012). PowerPoint Presentation in Arizona Department of Education Formative Assessment Professional Development Series Webinar, delivered April, 2, 2012.

system (see Figure 13.1). A balanced assessment system is a series of interacting assessments that provide the teacher and the learner information about educational growth.

Not all assessments are used for the same purpose and their goals vary as well (Heritage, Vendlinski, & Herman, 2009). In any balanced assessment system, each type of assessment has a purpose and expectations of use. These expectations can vary depending on whether the user is the teacher, the student, the principal, or district personnel.

Using multiple sources of data tends to better confirm hunches of what students are or are not learning and better inform stakeholders when making educational decisions. Relying on only one assessment and only one set of results to make decisions about student learning or teacher performance is contrary to best practices.

Within a balanced assessment system, assessing occurs at specific times to show what a student does or doesn't know and includes *diagnostic, the formative assessment process,* and *summative assessments.*

DIAGNOSTIC ASSESSMENTS

Diagnostics (sometimes referred to as *pre-assessments*) are used to assess prior knowledge of a topic or subject and to understand where students are entering the learning progression for an intended concept or content standards. A diagnostic is given at a point in time and is the sum of knowledge a student has before they embark on new learning. This type of assessment is given before the learning begins and should *not* be used for grading purposes (McMillan, 2000). The purpose of using a diagnostic assessment is to create a baseline to understand what knowledge students already know or what knowledge students are lacking about a topic or subject. Results should be used to address key concepts that will be needed for the new material to be learned (Wiggins, 1998). A solid diagnostic will focus on the essential knowledge of the unit, not trivial content.

THE FORMATIVE ASSESSMENT PROCESS

The formative assessment process, or AfL, is a process that takes place in the classroom instruction as students and teachers are intentionally moving toward a learning goal. It is the real-time adjustments or processes a teacher makes while instructing a class to ensure that the students are learning the content, keeping pace, and the learning progresses (Heritage, 2010). Refer back to Figure 13.1; this formative assessment process can take place minute by minute, daily, and/or weekly within the classroom instruction.

The formative assessment process might make more sense if one thinks of it as "formative instruction" or the "formative use of assessment information" (Good, 2011). What information is the teacher using to alter the growth of the student in the moment of teaching and learning? It's the reason for assessing—to evaluate for the purposes of adjusting instruction per student need—that makes it a formative assessment process.

These adjustments can be as simple as restating a fact, repeating an answer, or modeling a skill one more time. They can be as complex as taking a completely different approach to the concept, which could include the addition of peer teaching, small group instruction, alternative instructional strategies, or spending more time on a topic (Heritage, Vendlinski, & Herman, 2009).

Again, what makes assessing formative are the adjustments a teacher makes in response to evidence (blank stares, wrong answers, the look of confusion), but it also includes the *feedback* teachers give students in response to evidence (their work or product) and the student's *self-assessment* based on evidence (the student saying, "I get this, but not that," or using a rubric to rate their own work so the teacher can adjust the teaching and learning). The key word is "evidence." The teacher is continuously looking for immediate evidence that the students are learning, and the teacher is adjusting instruction based on the evidence.

The formative assessment process (if implemented well) not only trains students to self-assess and learn how to learn, but may also lead to efficiency in instructional time as teachers understand how the formative assessment process fits into a balanced system of assessment. Teachers are not wasting time re teaching concepts after the lesson is over because they are intentionally designing in lessons ways to catch the roadblocks and tackle misconceptions in the moment by planning to formatively assess the class.

Formative assessment strategies are designed for teachers and students to readily observe the evidence of learning. These strategies can include short prompts, learning logs, short problems, personal whiteboards, quick writes, or small group discussions, which provide a window into the learner's mind to uncover thinking. The Internet is full of formative assessment strategies. The prearranged strategies are intentionally placed within a lesson or unit when the teacher needs to check for understanding. These strategies reveal a student's thinking to let the teacher know if they need to slow down or pick up the pace of the lesson, differentiate for students who are not yet at conceptual understanding, or accelerate the learning if students show evidence that they are ready for the next level.

There are five essential elements to the formative assessment process (Heritage, 2010):

1. Identifying the gap between where the students are and where they should be, as well as what instruction will help close the gap and what it means to achieve success.
2. Providing feedback. In the formative assessment realm, this feedback should be a constant exchange between the student and the teacher.
3. Increasing active engagement in the student's learning process. The students must be engaged in and aware of their learning to let the teacher know what they know or don't know.
4. Creating progressions in learning. There need to be checks within the progress of the learning so that the teacher can make sure the students are not lost, or so the teacher can know when some students are starting to fall behind or are accelerating more quickly. This will assist the teacher when helping those students with scaffolds or opportunities to move all students forward in the learning progression.
5. Intentionally designing and using strategies to create opportunities to gather evidence of learning. Evidence of learning provides the window into the learner's thinking and allows for specific and targeted feedback.

Once these elements are in place, the feedback provided after reviewing the formative assessment data, which we will call *formative feedback*, needs to meet two criteria to be effective (Hattie & Timperley, 2007). One, it needs to be precise and directly help the student correct the mistake or perform the skill correctly. The feedback needs to drive a purposeful interaction between the teacher and the student so the student can make sense of the comments, express their thinking, and problem-solve based on the feedback provided (Linquanti, 2014).

Two, formative feedback needs to guide or offer the student a way of confirming their performance or ways to increase the performance. For example, a teacher might say, *"Tell me how you thought through this problem of dividing your half of the pizza into equal pieces to feed three more people. Think about the entire pizza. Using manipulatives fraction pieces, if you divided the other half of the pizza just like this one, how many pieces would you have? That's right, three more pieces. So how many pieces would be in the entire pizza? That's right, 6 altogether. So when you had a half divided by 3, they would each only have 1/6 of the entire pizza to eat."*

The example above consists of the teacher listening as well as speaking. If the teacher isn't listening and is only talking and not letting the student respond, then this teachable moment is lost. As with any relationship, it is key to listen. The relationship between the teacher and the student is no different.

Effective formative feedback should provide enough information for the student to understand where they are, where they need to be, as well as how to get there. With the use of feedback, the student can place new information with schemata formed by previous knowledge, and therefore make the connections needed to learn the new skill or concept. Good teachers provide feedback frequently and make sure the feedback is specific to the skills of the student.

Feedback must be provided in a timely manner and must state specifically what the student did right as well as how they can improve (Heritage, 2010). Marking a paper "good" or "needs improvement" is *not* specific feedback. If effective, formative feedback has been provided, the students should know exactly how to make the product better and can measure their own progress (Baleni, 2015). The student should be able to read the comments and understand what needs improvement, or understand what was specifically done correctly. Feedback is an essential way to increase student learning and provide the student with the knowledge needed to improve performance.

Formative feedback needs to focus on items necessary to master the skill and is significant to student growth. Educators have limited time with students and need to use this time wisely. When dialoguing with students about their performance, focus on things that count and can be applied in new situations (Black & Wiliam, 1998).

Feedback should *not* be stated as a judgment. Feedback needs to be presented objectively. It should be consistent and based on some form of evaluation, not an opinion. For students who are struggling or don't seem attached to school, try to point out more things they did well at first to show them that although they are struggling, they are improving and making gains. When reinforcing the positive,

- restate the objective or purpose of the assignment;
- give clear and specific examples from the assignment where the student achieved the objective or purpose of the assignment; and
- reinforce the student achievement by explaining exactly why sections of the assignment or skill met the objective of the lesson.

After pointing out the correct items, provide the students with areas in which they can improve and show them what they can do to improve. When providing ways for refinement, do the following:

- Prioritize the areas of refinement that are most important. Make sure to focus only on one or two areas of refinement. Focusing on too many areas of refinement can cause the students to lose faith in their ability to achieve the required result.
- Restate the objective or purpose of the assignment.
- Provide clear evidence as to why the area of refinement does not meet the objective.
- Provide clear examples of how the students can make the area of refinement meet the objective.
- Provide an opportunity for the students to refine the area, or have the students say in their own words how they could improve the area of refinement in future assignments.

Please note: When planning lessons, a teacher has to plan for this additional time. Not only does the learner need time to implement the refinement; the teacher needs time to give immediate feedback on the student's corrective work.

The last key part, and probably the most important aspect of formative assessment, is empowering the students to self-assess their own work. An effective teacher creates a classroom culture where it is okay to make a mistake. When asking students to assess what they know, the teacher needs to (A) create a safe classroom atmosphere in which students know their admittance of not knowing something will be used only to help them learn it, not to be scored and decrease a grade; and (B) show the students what they are supposed to know (Heritage, 2010).

For the first part, if students feel they will get an F if they don't understand the content immediately, they might not be open to explore where they are in the learning process. The teacher needs to explain that the purpose of self-assessment within formative assessment is for the teacher to help. These self-assessments are *never* graded.

Secondly, the teacher needs to help the student understand the final product/skill level, so the students knows if they are at an appropriate level of understanding. This can best be done with rubrics, exemplars, or good samples of previous student work. Effective teachers let students reflect on their own work and provide the students will a self-assessment rubric or reflective questions to help guide the students in their thinking (Bandura, 1997). This creates the environment for formative assessment to become deeply rooted, to thrive and to grow.

Formative feedback can come in many forms including written, verbal, or electronic. With the advancements of technology, formative assessment can be utilized in virtual classes or by itinerant teachers. No matter the format, the key elements remain the same: the feedback is specific, thorough, and not judgmental.

The formative assessment process is the foundation of learning; however, there is a place for assessing after a unit is completed or the school year is complete. This is assessing *of* learning or summative assessment.

SUMMATIVE ASSESSMENT

Summative assessment is used to evaluate student learning at the beginning and at the end of an instructional unit, a semester, or a year. Summatives can be used as a diagnostics. The most common summative assessments are end-of-chapter tests, end-of-course tests, end-of-year exams, state assessments, national assessments, and international assessments. End-of-chapter or end-of-course assessments are often graded and used for accountability. Summative assessments should necessitate the application of skills, concepts, and understandings. Summative assessments are also administered to ensure that a curriculum is aligned to learning standards.

When looking at summative assessment data, the educator should ask the following questions:

- What evidence do I have that shows the knowledge, skills, and understandings our students have achieved for the year?
- What evidence do I have that the curriculum implemented and taught was aligned to the educational standards for the state, district, and school or department?
- Which data indicate the degree to which my students show the conceptual understandings and generalizations in our standards?
- What evidence shows which students are meeting or exceeding our achievement expectations and which are not?
- What do I know about how each individual student learns?

When summatively assessing knowledge or skills, if possible, choices ought to be provided to the class (Kellough & Kellough, 1999). Students should be given the chance to work to their strengths or choose how they will demonstrate the knowledge, skill, or understanding to the teacher. If the teacher provides a list of evidence needed from the student to show mastery of a concept, why not let the student decide in which form the evidence will be provided?

Interim assessments, sometimes called benchmark assessments, are a type of summative assessment administered to students periodically throughout the year, usually quarterly, at a planned time. Interim assessments are instruments used to see how a student is performing academically (Stiggins, 2008). The most common purpose for interim/benchmark assessments is to understand student learning of a segment of material, or period of time. The results are often used as a prediction on how students will fare on an end-of-the-year summative assessment.

Many people often confuse interim assessment with formative assessment (Perie, Marion, & Gong, 2009). Most likely, if a school or district says they have purchased a formative assessment program, in reality they have probably bought an interim assessment program. Interim assessments can technically be used in the formative assessment process if the data from the interim assessment is used to change instructional decisions by the teacher.

As mentioned so far in this chapter, assessments vary and are designed and built for a purpose. Diagnostics are given in the beginning of a lesson or unit to see what students already know. The formative assessment process uses strategies to assess students informally throughout the lesson to drive the learning and alter instruction. Summative assessments are given at the end of learning. If used together properly, a balanced assessment system is created and will provide stakeholders with reliable and valid results to inform educational decisions. Rick Stiggins (2017) provides a framework for planning a balanced assessment system (see Figure 13.2).

WHAT TO ASSESS?

So what does a teacher need to assess and to what degree? Research suggests that teachers should use an assessment map or a blueprint to ensure that the assessment not only covers the standards but also offers a broad range of thinking, including higher-order thinking (Brookhart, 2010). Most assessment maps contain the content, or the topic being assessed, as well as the cognitive domain of Bloom's Taxonomy (Anderson et al., 2001). This allows the teacher to map out the assessment and check to make sure more than one domain is being assessed (see Figure 13.3).

Level \ Type of Assessment	Formative Classroom Assessment	Formative--Assessment FOR Learning	Summative Applications
Classroom Assessment • Key decision maker(s) • Important instructional decisions to be made • Information needed to inform decisions	Teacher What comes next in my students' learning? Standards setting clear and appropriate learning progressions Evidence of standards mastered and not yet and types of problems students are having	Student/teacher team Student: What comes next in my learning? Can I master it? Student-friendly standards placed learning progressions Diagnostic evidence of student's current place in progressions and of problems students are having	Teacher What grade or standards mastered go on report cards? Evidence of student mastery of each required standard
Periodic Benchmark Tests • Key decision maker(s) • Instructional decisions to be made • Information needed to inform decisions	Curriculum and Instructional leaders, teacher teams, PLCs Which standards are our students struggling mastering and what can we do about it? Evidence of standards covered but not mastered by all or most students	Teachers; but students can assist in interpreting results Which standards do I tend to struggle mastering and why? Evidence of standards I have failed to master `	Curriculum and Instructional leaders Which standards are broad samples of our student not mastering? Evidence of standards mastered across broad samples using common assessments
Annual Tests • Key decision maker(s) • Instructional decisions • Information needed	Results must reveal how each student has done in mastering each standard Curriculum and instructional leaders What required standards did our students not master? Evidence of require (expected) standards mastered or not?	There is no assessment FOR learning role of annual tests	District leadership team, school board and community Did enough of our students master required standards? Evidence of the proportion of our students mastering each standard

Figure 13.2   Instructional Decision Framework Addressed in a Balanced Assessment System From Chappuis, S., Commodore, C., & Stiggins, R. (2017). *Balanced assessment systems: Leadership, quality, and the role of classroom assessment.* Permission is granted by the author for CCSSO FAST-SCASS members to share this chart.

For a beginning teacher, using an assessment map can make creating assessments easier. After a while, the teacher will begin to remember which verbs (define, identify, distinguish, etc.) belong to which cognitive domain, and the use of the assessment map might become more infrequent. Each stakeholder group needs to consider what information they need from the assessment to make the best informed educational decisions. Understanding what educational decisions they will make and what information must be gathered to make them is what is meant by *assessment data literacy*. What hunches do stakeholders have concerning learning and what type of assessment will provide the information needed to get information to determine next steps in planning for the improvement of the learning?

So what are the educational questions teachers should ask when creating an assessment? How will principals, teachers, parents, and students use the

DIMENSION	DEFINITION	EXAMPLES
REMEMBER	*Promoting retention of the presented material in much of the same form as it was taught*	
Recognizing	Locating knowledge in long-term memory is consistent with presented material	True or False. The attack on Pearl Harbor occurred in 1941. How many sides does a triangle have? A) 1 B) 2 C) 3
Recalling	Recalling relevant knowledge from long term memory when given a prompt to so do	On what date did the attack on Pearl Harbor occur? How many sides does a triangle have?
UNDERSTAND	*Construct meaning from instructional messages, including oral, written, and graphic communication*	
Interpreting	Converting information from one representational form to another	Draw a picture of the checks and balances system in government. Explain in your own words how the system works.
Exemplifying	Giving specific examples, an instance of defining the features of a general concept or principle	Give an example of a dangling modifier. Which of the following is a mammal: crow, salmon, or bacteria?
Classifying	Recognizing that something belongs to a certain category or detecting relevant features/patterns that fit the concept or principle	Sort the following numbers based on whether they are a polynomial or a monomial.
Summarizing	Suggesting a single statement that represents information or abstracts a general theme	Write a statement summarizing the plot of the story "The Necklace."
Inferring	Finding a pattern within a series of examples and inducing a pattern based on given information or a series of examples	) Which number do you think comes next in this series: 3, 6, 12, 24? Based on the end of Chapter 3, what do you predict will happen in Chapter 4?

Figure 13.3 Bloom's Taxonomy. Adapted from Anderson, L. W., & Krathwohl, D. (2001). *A taxonomy for learning, teaching, and assessing: A revision of Bloom's taxonomy of educational objectives.*

Comparing	Detecting similarities and differences between two or more objects, events, ideas, problems, or situations	Describe how the two experiments were alike and different. Using the diagram, explain the similarities and differences between the Catholic and Mormon religions.
Explaining	Constructing and/or using a cause-effect model of a system	Explain how a liquid becomes a gas.
APPLY	*Using procedures to perform exercises or solve problems*	
Executing	Carrying out a procedure when given a familiar task/exercise	Using the demonstrated procedure, execute an effective bench press. Using the Pythagorean theorem…
Implementing	Selecting and using a procedure to perform an unfamiliar task/exercise	Solve the following word problem.
ANALYZE	*Breaking a concept into its constituent parts and determining how the parts are related to one another and to an overall structure*	
Differentiating	Distinguishing the parts of a whole structure in terms of their relevance or importance	Read the following story and decide which information is relevant and which is not relevant.
Organizing	Building systematic and coherent connections among pieces of information	Prepare an outline for your report.
Attributing	Ascertaining the point of view, biases, values, or intention underlying communication	What do you think is the purpose of this editorial?
EVALUATE	*Making judgments based on clearly defined criteria and standards*	
Checking	Testing for internal inconsistencies or fallacies	What are possible problems with Marxism? Based on the argument, what inconsistencies are present in the argument?

Figure 13.3 (Continued)

results? Before answering these questions, teachers should refer to three key principles: (1) consider albums versus snapshots, (2) align the measurement to match it with the goal, and (3) ensure that form follows function (Forster & Masters, 2004).

Critiquing	Judging a product or operation based on externally imposed criteria and standards	Based on the 6 Traits Scoring Rubric, score the following paper on conventions and organization.
CREATE	***Putting elements together to form a coherent or functional whole. It may or may not include originality or uniqueness. It is drawing upon elements from many sources and putting them together into a structure or pattern relative to one's own prior knowledge.***	
Generating	Redefining, arriving at alternatives or hypotheses that meet certain criteria	List plausible alternatives to gasoline as a fuel.
Planning	Developing a solution when given a problem	List the steps you will use to correctly build a functional kitchen cabinet system.
Producing	Carrying out a plan for solving a given problem that meets certain specifications	Build a functional kitchen cabinet system.

Figure 13.3 (Continued)

Consider Photo Albums versus Snapshots

Multiple sources of evidence are more reliable than "one shot" snapshots. A variety of classroom assessments can show a teacher, student, and parents if any progress has been made throughout the day, unit, week, or even semester. A variety of assessments is important from a measurement perspective but also as a matter of sensitivity to varied learners.

Align the Measures to Match with the Goals

Students shouldn't be surprised by the assessment; it should be a natural way for them to show what they know based on what was taught. Per Thomas Guskey, "Assessments reflect the concepts and skills that the teacher emphasized in class, along with the teacher's clear criteria for judging students' performance" (Guskey, 2003). Let the student know what will be assessed.

Bear in mind that there is a difference between *knowing* (either you know it or you don't) and *understanding* (the degree one can explain, interpret, apply, have perspective, display empathy, and show meta cognitive awareness). For collecting appropriate evidence of learning, create projects or scenarios using the GRASPS acronym (Wiggins & McTighe, 1999):

Goal: "Your task or goal is to create/write . . ."
Role: "Approach this as though you are a . . ." "Make believe that you are a _____, and create it from that point of view."
Audience: "Your audience is. . ."

Situation: "Your challenge is to take this point of view . . . " "Your challenge is to use only these materials . . ."
Product/performance: "You will create a . . ." You will write a . . ."
Standards: "Your performance needs to meet these criteria . . ."

Form Follows Function

The design and use of classroom assessments should be influenced by three questions: What is being assessed, why is it being assessed, and how will the results be used and by whom? Start with the end in mind. Based on the standards, what does the teacher want the students to know and be able to do? Let this guide the teaching. What kind of information does the teacher need that will help students determine where they are in the learning progression, and what does the teacher need to do to assist them in climbing to the next level?

It could be to target the student's *knowledge* or recall: "Name the capital of New Mexico."

It could be to target the student's *reasoning*: "If two trains are heading to Texas and one is going 50 mph, the other is going 75 mph . . ."

It could be to target the student's *performance:* "Run one mile in under nine minutes."

It could be to target the student's development of a *product:* "Cook a chocolate cake using the recipe we learned this week."

To have a clear target, take three things into consideration (Smaldino, Lowther, & Russell, 2007):

1. *Conditions:* Define the materials available. "After reading the story Othello . . ."
2. *Behavior:* What will the student do? This has a verb: solve, compare, and so on.
3. *Criterion or degree:* How will the teacher know if it is achieved? What will be measured?

Once the conditions, behavior, and criterion are taken into consideration, a clear assessment target is achieved. An example of a target would be, "After reading the play *Othello*, the student will compare three character traits of Iago and Othello."

Assessment items like true/false, fill-in-the-blank, and multiple choice are called *selected response items*, or *closed tasks*. With selected response items, each question has a right and wrong answer and can be impartially scored. These are good to use if the teacher wants the students to only recall information or identify facts or concepts. As assessment author Erik Francis states, these types of questions rarely measure cognitive complexity and do not "indicate that students truly learned the concept or content as deeply as they should" (Francis, 2016). It is important to note from Bloom's Taxonomy which cognitive level is being addressed; the teacher does not want all the questions to be at the lower level of thinking skills.

Selected response items are usually very easy to grade (students can get immediate feedback), they're objective (teacher's preferences do not influence the result), and can often be used year after year. The drawback to these items is they aren't very engaging, can often be busy work, can often provide incorrect data (what if the kid picked the right true/false answer by luck, not by knowledge?), and aren't process based (they are based on content). Items like these are fine to use in moderation, but don't fall into the trap of handing out worksheets every day or use for every final exam.

When using multiple choice, up the ante by offering "distractors." Distractors are wrong answers that look like they could be right and can also be used to inform a teacher as to what the student doesn't understand. For example, let's look at this simple mathematics problem:

$2 + 5 \times 2 = ?$

A. *12*
B. *14*
C. *9*
D. *11*

The correct answer is A, 12. Based on the distractors, if a student answered B, the teacher would know the student made an order of operations mistake and added 2 + 5 first and then multiplied by 2. If the student answered C, the teacher could assume the student added all the numbers and didn't multiply. By making sure that at least two or more options are incorrect with a reason, the teacher can use the data to address the student's misunderstanding of the content. If the other wrong answer options were unrealistic, like (A) 12, (B) 2000, (C) 0, (D) 1,000,001, the teacher would have no way of assessing the student's mistake.

When writing a multiple-choice question, make sure all the answers seem like they could be the correct answer and make sure they are similarly grouped. Answers should also be similar in length and grammatical form.

For example: *The third President of the United States was:*

A. *Abraham Lincoln*
B. *Thomas Jefferson*
C. *Andrew Jackson*
D. *James Monroe*

As one can see, all the choices are presidents and they all served within the first ten terms. All the answers are similar in length.

Here's a nonexample: *The third President of the United States was:*

A. *Bart Simpson*
B. *Thomas Jefferson*

C. *President Andrew Jackson*
D. *Quarterback Kurt Warner*

In this example, only two are plausible answers and the group is not homogenous (two are presidents, one is an NFL Hall of Fame football player, and one is a cartoon character).

All assessment items should be well constructed so they actually measure what the student knows. For example, most multiple-choice questions have four answers. If a student gets the answer correct, is it because the student knew the answer, or is it that the student guessed and got lucky? In a four-answer multiple-choice question, there is a 25 percent chance the student could get the answer right without knowing the answer. One way to get around this is to require the students write a sentence about how they knew the answer was correct, or in mathematics, have the students show their work.

When creating a matching question, the same rules for the multiple-choice questions apply. Make sure the answers are homogenous, similar in length, and similar in grammatical form. Some teachers add more answers than questions. Having more answers than questions decreases the chance the student will guess the correct answer or use the process of elimination, not their knowledge, to get to an answer.

When writing true/false items within an assessment, ensure the statements are completely true or completely false. If they aren't, confusion will occur. Try not to use "always" or "never." These words are dead giveaways to students who are test savvy that the answer is probably false.

Here's an example: *True or False: Andrew Jackson vetoed the renewal of the national bank charter.*

In this example, the statement is completely true and is clear.

Here's a nonexample: *True or False: Andrew Jackson always vetoed anything that had to do with national rights over states' rights because states' rights allowed for him to extend his wealth.*

This nonexample is confusing and is not completely true. Jackson was pro-states' rights, but the reasons varied, and a historian could most likely find an instance in which he didn't veto a measure that supported national power.

Another type of assessment item is the *open response assessment*, also called the *constructed response assessment*. It might provide a sentence stem, or pose a question, and will offer many different forms of responses. This type of assessment question makes the students process information, interpret their learning, and provide evidence and reasoning behind their answers. It takes longer to grade than the closed task assessment mentioned above, but it does provide more evidence of what the child really learned. An essay or extended response would fall under this category. The following are two examples of open response questions:

The Industrial Revolution had a deep effect on human history. In your opinion, what was the most important innovation during this time? Explain why you think it had the biggest impact on this time period.

The Women's Rights Movement had an impact on America by . . .

Fill-in-the-blank questions are probably the most common constructed response item used in education. When creating a fill-in-the-blank question, make sure the question has a definite answer and have only one blank per item.

For example: *The third President of the United States was: _____.*

In this example, there is only one correct answer, Thomas Jefferson.

Here is a nonexample: *The _____ President of the _____ _____ was _____.*

In this nonexample, based on the number of blanks, many different sentences could be completed that may be a correct statement, although not the one the teacher was looking for.

Essay questions are another good way of ensuring if a student truly knows the answer. Essays are a much deeper type of constructed response assessment. A prompt for an essay question should explain exactly how a student is to respond and should emphasize higher-level thinking.

Example: *Based on three current news articles, create an exit plan for the United States to leave Iraq. Include political, military, and economic solutions.*

In this example, the students are told specifically what to focus on and the essay prompt emphasizes more than just recall of facts.

Nonexample: *Write about getting the United States out of Iraq.*

In this nonexample, the poorly written essay prompt is vague and leaves a lot to be desired.

Some students are better writers than others, and a poor essay response due to limited writing skills can downplay what a student actually knows about the subject, while vivid and rich writing skills can mask misunderstanding. Also, if you rely on essay questions, make sure to use a rubric to grade the essay to communicate to students expectations for full points and also to ensure all essays are scored fairly and objectively. As any honest teacher will admit, if grading 40–50 essay questions and not using a rubric, there is a great chance that as grading becomes cumbersome, the overall scores will either decline or increase, and if the last essay graded is held next to the first graded two hours ago, there could be inconsistencies. Rubrics are discussed in detail later in this chapter.

Performance tasks are a great way for students to show procedural knowledge. With a performance task, the student actually does something. For example, "*Show me how to clean a carburetor.*" "*Use the scientific method to solve . . .*"

Journals are another way to assess what a student knows. Having students write about what they know about a topic before and after a lesson can help the teacher to assess growth. Based on the entries, the teacher can see what the students retained as well as any misinformation they might have.

A student-to-teacher interview can be used as an assessment item. Although time consuming, these provide an open conversation about learning and can bring a lot to the table. In these academic interviews, the teacher sits down with an individual student and asks specific questions about a certain subject. For example, "We've been talking about plot lately. What can you tell me about the plot of *Romeo and Juliet*?"

No matter what type of assessment items are utilized, use the assessment data to provide focus for improving teacher instruction. Patterns within the data will create targets or a pathway for instructional strategies, as well as the effectiveness of those strategies. By reflecting on assessment data, an educator, a student, or a parent can see trends in the feedback and decide to "stay the course" or if changes need to occur.

ASSESSMENT VERSUS GRADING

In many classrooms and schools across the country, grading is pretty much the professional judgment call of the teacher (Guskey, 2000). Basically, if it is up to the teacher to decide what constitutes an A, B, C, D, or F then the grade is based on the opinion of the individual teacher. When students receive varying grades across teachers and schools based on the same artifact of work, *differential grading* takes place. Differential grading can occur due to stereotypes, teacher quality, grading standards, or behavior (Rauschenberg, 2014). Educators need to avoid differential grading at all costs.

Although all teachers tend to grade something, rarely do they talk to each other about its purpose. Grading seems to be one of those things never questioned in the field of education; it has been handed down by the elders of this profession so teachers do it without ever asking "Why do we do this? Are we all on the same page? Are we all basing our grades on the same factors?"

During one of the author's first year as a teacher, grading seemed to be something that piled up and he'd find himself grading papers while eating dinner or watching television. It wasn't until he had his first parent-teacher conference that he began to question his grading practices. The conference was for a student who was getting a D in the class, and they endlessly butted heads during class. Well, the student's parents were not happy—with the author! For an hour he had to justify the grades he had given this student as well as explain how this student fared compared to other students in the class. Could the author prove that the student's grade was based on his performance and not the sour relationship?

The author second-guessed how he graded after that conference because one thing became apparent: he did not have a way of ensuring that he graded all the student work the same way with the same expectations, and when asked, he couldn't provide a set of criteria to justify his grading system. If he gave a paper an A, and if it was snuck back into the grading pile, could he ensure that he'd give it an A again, and based on the same criteria? If someone randomly placed an A paper and a B paper in front of him, could he state the differences to justify the difference in grades? From that day on he took grading more seriously and searched for a more systematic way of doing it.

A scoring rubric is a tool containing criteria and a performance scale that allows us to systematically define and describe the most important components that comprise complex performances and products (Arter & McTighe, 2001). Items that comprise of complex performances and products need a tool to ensure that grading is consistent for each portion of the performance or product. When created and applied correctly, a rubric can improve not just evaluation, but also instruction and motivation (Gasaymeh, 2011).

A rubric is not a checklist. A checklist only shows if something is included or not included; it's more of a "yes/no" tool than a rubric. A checklist does not provide levels of performance or a rating. For example, here is a checklist for a business letter (Figure 13.4):

Key Elements	yes	no
The letter contains the sender's address.		
The letter contains the recipient's name and address.		
The month is written out, and the letter includes the day and year in the date.		
The first letter of the salutation is capitalized.		
A colon is placed after the recipient's name is the salutation.		
The first body paragraph clearly explains why the letter is being written.		
The letter follows consistent block form.		
The closing body paragraph restates the letter's purpose.		
Only the first word of the closing is capitalized.		
A comma follows the closing.		
The business letter has a formal tone.		

Figure 13.4   Business Letter Checklist

As one can see, in the checklist, there is no degree of success; it is just a matter of the item being either present or not. This is okay for basic tasks, but once the assignment gets more complex, a checklist will no longer suffice.

Rubrics assist in consistency of scoring. They help the teacher refrain from personal judgment and assist him/her in scoring a paper or performance based on the rubric's criteria and predefined criteria.

Rubrics can help the teacher and student by clarifying the goal of the product or performance and the targets the student needs to focus on for quality. The rubric explains what qualities differ between a poor assignment and a quality assignment. The students know what qualities are expected for an A paper, and there is a better chance they will include these qualities within their work.

The number of traits in a rubric really doesn't matter, but should be reflective of the number of important parts of the assessment. The most important thing is that each trait focuses on a central part of the product or skill and that trivial items aren't added just for the sake of adding more traits to the rubric. Most rubrics have a scale score between 4 and 6. The scale score really doesn't matter either, just as long as there are enough points to adequately distinguish different forms of quality.

A *generic rubric* can be used across various tasks. An example of a generic rubric is provided below (Figure 13.5).

One problem with this rubric is although it provides a scale, it does not define what is needed for each score. Depending on the assignment and how long the teacher has been teaching the specific group of students, a vague, generic rubric may or may not be appropriate. In the example above, the

Attribute	You	Teacher
The beginning paragraph evidently tells what the writer will be discussing	1 2 3 4 5	1 2 3 4 5
All additional paragraphs relate to the topic	1 2 3 4 5	1 2 3 4 5
The length is a minimum of one page long	1 2 3 4 5	1 2 3 4 5
Complete sentences are applied throughout the essay	1 2 3 4 5	1 2 3 4 5
Sentences differ in length	1 2 3 4 5	1 2 3 4 5
All sentences do not start with the identical words	1 2 3 4 5	1 2 3 4 5
All sentences are comprehendible	1 2 3 4 5	1 2 3 4 5
Descriptive words are used	1 2 3 4 5	1 2 3 4 5
Slang words are not utilized in the essay, unless used in dialog	1 2 3 4 5	1 2 3 4 5
Overused, cliché words have been replaced with more interesting words	1 2 3 4 5	1 2 3 4 5

Figure 13.5 Generic Rubric

student would have to already know what constitutes a score of a 4 or a score of a 5. What's nice about this rubric is it has a "you" section where the student scores himself/herself before submitting the assignment to the teacher, and then a "teacher" area where the teacher can score it. The "you" section could also be modified to say "peer," allowing a classmate to score the paper first, and then the student would take the peer's input and make necessary revisions and refinements before submitting it for a final grade. Peer-based evaluation has been found to be very effective in assisting students to be more attentive to their improvement rather than simply motivating students for a certain grade (Kinne, Hasenbank, & Coffey, 2014).

See Figure 13.6 for a more thorough generic rubric.

In this example, each score point is specifically spelled out. This prevents the teacher from using their judgment and keeps the teacher scoring the paper objectively. This would be considered a generic rubric because it could be used for any type of writing assignment.

	4	3	2	1
Content	Contains numerous relevant facts and details; the assignment requirements for specific content choices are thoroughly met.	Contains adequate facts and details to complete the assignment, content choice is met but limited.	Some facts and details are present; although some are also missing. Not all content choices are within the assignment.	Facts and details are missing; content choices do not reflect the assignment.
Organization	Includes catchy introduction; logically sequenced paragraphs with transitions; strong conclusion that reiterates the main point.	Contains an introduction; adequately developed paragraphs and a couple clear transitions; conclusion is present.	Logical organization; introduction and conclusion are not fully developed; transitions are missing.	Poor organization; facts and details are stated without paragraphs or transitions; introduction and conclusion are missing.
Construction	Sentence construction is varied; spelling and punctuation are correct; sentences flow seamlessly.	A few examples of varied sentence construction; few errors in spelling and punctuation; sentences flow, although some choppy sentences are present.	Repetitive sentence construction; some spelling and punctuation errors distract the reader; choppy sentences distract the reader.	Sentence construction errors are present, many spelling and punctuation errors distract the reader and make the writing impossible to finish.

Figure 13.6 Thorough Generic Rubric

	3	2	1
In tune	All strings are in tune following the EADGBE standard tuning.	Most of the strings are in tune following the EADGBE standard tuning.	None of the strings are in tune and don't follow the EADGBE standard tuning.
Nut/Pegs	All six strings are correctly placed on the nut and correctly wound in the peg.	Most of the six strings are correctly placed on the nut and are adequately wound in the peg.	None of the six strings are correctly placed on the nut or correctly wound in the peg.

Figure 13.7 Task-Specific Rubric

A *task-specific rubric* (Figure 13.7) lives up to its name; it can be used only for one specific task. For example, the following rubric could be used for tuning a guitar, but probably not much else (it couldn't be used for tuning a piano or other instrument).

In this example, the rubric really can't be used for anything but tuning a guitar. It can't even be used for other instruments, like a piano. Because of this, it would be considered a task-specific rubric.

The use of rubrics benefits all students and can be a very effective support for students with disabilities. A rubric can be accommodated for individualization, for example, to align to a student's IEP goal or objective. The rubric can also be given to the struggling student prior to the rest of the class, therefore providing the teacher additional time to clearly explain the grading criteria and answer any specific questions.

ACCESS FOR ALL STUDENTS

Remember that when assessing learning for students with a disability, accommodations and modifications might be required to ensure students have access to the test. Based on the children and what is stated in their IEP, these accommodations or modifications are put in place to remove factors that, due to the student's disability, would prevent the assessment from measuring the child's content knowledge.

Accommodations, defined as "changes in instruction or assessment practices that reduce the impact of an individual's disability on his/her interaction with the material," can include changes to the setting, seating, time, format, method, or materials used (Ketterlin-Geller & Johnstone, 2006). Accommodations such as extended time, items being read aloud, chunking directions, allowing for verbal responses, or test items being translated by an interpreter would not invalidate the assessment and still allow the student to participate in the assessment. Accommodations don't "dumb-down" the material or the assessment; they merely alter the delivery mode so the student can participate. With accommodations, the test is still measuring the same knowledge and skills at the appropriate rigor and grade level.

Modifications, unlike accommodations, will change what the test is measuring or will modify the rigor or expectation. Modifications can include lowering the level of understanding required, simplifying vocabulary or concepts, altering grading, or changing assessment items.

The child's IEP team (which, at a minimum, should include the parents, school administrator, special education teacher, general education teacher, and someone who can interpret evaluation results) decides which accommodations or modifications will be included for that student. It is not up to the individual teacher to decide when accommodations and modifications should or should not be in place. If it is written in the student's IEP, it is a legal expectation that the modification or accommodation is used as stated.

One way to approach assessment in a manner that works for all kids is to provide students more independence and personalization by including the principles of universal design for learning (UDL). Per author Sally Spencer, UDL is "the proactive application of instructional design concepts, pedagogical knowledge, and instructional technology to create instruction that is accessible and engaging to learners across the spectrum of ability" (Spencer, 2011). This basically means the teacher designs an assessment that works universally (for all students), no matter what their abilities are. The term "UDL" is referenced many times in the Every Student Succeeds Act (ESSA) and over the past decade has been seen as a way to inclusively deliver content and skills in a manner that is accessible to all students.

Unfortunately, in most U.S. classrooms an assessment is produced that requires all students to create the same output as evidence that content was learned. For example, a social studies teacher might ask the class to write an essay about current conflicts in the Middle East as a way to assess what they have learned about recent global conflicts. Here is the problem: This assignment is equally focused on assessing how well the student is able to adhere to the conventions of writing an essay as it is focused on assessing the student's understanding of conflicts in that part of the world. For a student who has a specific learning disability in reading or writing, it is not a fair way of assessing what the student knows about current conflicts in the Middle East.

When teachers eliminate the construct-irrelevant factors (factors that distract from what is actually being assessed) from assessments, they will get a more precise picture of what knowledge, skills, and abilities students are actually achieving. In the scenario above, the tenants of UDL could be applied by the social studies teacher providing the differentiation of assessment possibilities to the class, such as choosing an option of either giving a verbal explanation of the causes of conflicts in the Middle East, creating a graph and timeline, creating a video, writing a paper, etc.

Employing universal design in all types of assessing (diagnostic, the formative assessment process, and summative) is one way to evaluate what the student knows without including construct-irrelevant factors that offer only one output. Universal design is revolutionizing assessment by providing equity in access and removing barriers for all types of learners.

REFLECTION SCENARIO

Mr. Smith is teaching a 40-minute introductory lesson on the parts of a plant cell. He has gone over the diagram of the plant cell on the board with the students, has had them label the parts of the cell, and write the functions of each part of the cell in their science journals. He asks them to close their journals and points to parts of the cell diagram on the board and asks who knows what the name of this part is and what function it serves. Students raise their hands and he calls on one student at a time to name the part and the function until all the parts have been named. There are 35 students in the class. He then moves on to cell reproduction. How will he know that all *of his students have learned the parts of the cell and functions before he moves on to the next concept? How would you assess the students for learning?*

Think about the last lesson you taught. How did you assess for learning? Is there anything you might want to change about your assessment strategies to make it more universally accessible? How did you know when the students were ready to move on to the next concept?

Chapter 14

Struggling Students
What Is an Intervention?

Humility and knowledge in poor clothes excel pride and ignorance in costly attire.

—William Penn

Year in and year out, dreaded end-of-year math and language arts exams stand as the supreme fear of many students who aren't testing at grade level. In 2015, 28 percent of twelfth graders remained at a below basic reading level, the lowest of four reading levels, and that figure did not include those who already dropped out due to poor literary skills (NAEP, 2015). For some students, exams are high stakes and can prevent students from graduating. But even when there are no high stakes exams, if students' needs aren't being met, they will fail.

This is where the importance of *interventions* come into play. An intervention is a program or strategy to assist a student in an area of need.

RESPONSE TO INTERVENTION

In most U.S. schools and districts, a system is in place to identify and track who needs an intervention and whether or not an intervention is being used. RTI, or Response to Intervention, is basically a problem-solving process in which teachers use data to make timely decisions about student success and decide which interventions need to be used with students who are starting to fall behind (Hall, 2008). RTI is based on the beliefs that preventative, early interaction is needed before students fail or need remediation; the use of universal screenings prevent students from "falling through the cracks."

RTI is considered a tiered system of supports. That means that there are different tiers, or levels, of support provided depending on what a child needs. All students will get an initial level of support (Tier 1), which is the universal instruction that takes place in the general education classroom. If data show some students are struggling academically, then in addition to Tier 1 instruction they will also receive additional support (Tier 2). This could include the student receiving targeted instruction in a smaller group with additional explicit instruction, additional tutoring, or including a supplemental reading curriculum, just to name a few examples. If data show that the Tier 2 interventions didn't work, then in addition to Tier 1 and Tier 2 instructions a third level of support (Tier 3) is applied. Tier 3 interventions are of longer duration, intensity, and individualization. Similarly to Tier 2, Tier 3 must supplement the Tier 1 core instruction (Harlacher, Sanford, & Nelson, 2014). We will go into more detail on each level of support later in this chapter.

A tiered system of supports can also help a school document what instructional practices are in place as well as help set targets for student growth (McInerney & Elledge, 2013). Because RTI is designed to identify struggling students, it can also be used to assist in identifying students who might have a disability. RTI is mentioned in federal law (Individuals with Disabilities Education Improvement Act) and the majority of U.S. states attempt to formally implement the method (McInerney & Elledge, 2013). The degree of successful RTI implementation in these states is a matter of debate.

The term RTI is sometimes incorrectly used interchangeably with MTSS, which stands for Multi-Tiered System of Supports. MTSS includes RTI (which focuses on academics) but also focuses on social, emotional, and behavioral development.

Before RTI, some students would fall far behind in school before anyone intervened, and sometimes that lack of a timely intervention would assist in making the student qualify for special education services. What RTI tries to do is quickly identify concerns so the issue can be corrected and the student can get back into the appropriate grade-level material. This process assists in making sure special education services are truly used for those students who need to receive additional services due to a disability. Why the need to intervene early in a child's educational career? Research shows that it takes four times as long to intervene in fourth grade as in late kindergarten to improve a student's skills by the same amount (Lyon, 1997).

RTI is a school-based or district-based effort. Never will a successful RTI program be based out of only one or two classrooms with no school or district support. The success of RTI truly depends on a reliable assessment tool that can identify students who are at risk and need intervention. To work effectively, MTSS and RTI both require collaboration between general education and special education teachers (Hurst, 2014; Tkatchov & DeVries, 2017).

As stated earlier in the chapter, there are three tiers of intervention. Tier 1 is basic, effective classroom instruction that all students in the class receive. Tier 1 instruction is the most important part of RTI, and all students should be engaged in this core instruction (Fuchs & Fuchs, 2005). Tier 1 assessments include items like end-of-unit tests and the universal screenings. Between 70 and 80 percent of the class should meet benchmark within the Tier 1 instruction. If this is not the case, there is a problem with Tier 1 core instruction, which could include the teaching strategies, the materials, and/or the overall curriculum.

As stated earlier, effective Tier 1 instruction is crucial to RTI and teamwork is essential. Teachers need to share expertise with colleagues to glean information from those having success with the core instruction and to share strategies with struggling colleagues to help them adjust instruction (Tkatchov & DeVries, 2017). The implementation of solid Tier 1 instruction takes time and in many cases requires a good core program.

Classroom teachers are key players in deciding if the core is taught successfully or not. Effective teachers get the most out of core instruction by including a mix of whole and small group instruction in which all students participate. They use the differentiation techniques discussed in chapters 4 and 8 to attend to individual student needs. Effective teachers make sure at-risk students are seated in the most appropriate place to effectively learn and provide all students with opportunities to practice new skills or apply new knowledge.

Quality Tier 1 instruction relies on the teacher using data to make decisions. Effective teachers review data often to assess how students are doing and, based on the data, differentiate and change instruction as needed.

For the students who do not meet benchmark in Tier 1, they are then provided Tier 2 interventions. These interventions are only for the students who did not meet benchmark and the interventions should only be used short term. These interventions are provided *in addition* to the Tier 1 instruction, not instead of Tier 1 instruction. In this tier, students are usually grouped by their deficits and small group instruction is provided by the teacher. In Tier 2, all activities are teacher directed. As in Tier 1, the teacher continues to collect data and uses the data to determine whether the student has made progress, whether the student has met the benchmark, or if the student is still not grasping the knowledge and skills that were taught.

For the students who still struggle in Tier 2, RTI has a final tier, Tier 3. As stated above, Tier 2 is to be used short term and is provided along with Tier 1. Students who still need more intervention can be placed in Tier 3, in which the focus is very intense. As RTI author Susan Hall states, "In Tier 3 the curriculum consists of a program in which the skills are arranged in a sequence- all skills are taught rather than just a few. Teachers use more modeling to show the task, and more scaffolding is provided" (Hall, 2008). The time allotted in Tier 3 should be double the time allotted in Tier 2, allowing for more repetition and specific teacher feedback.

TYPES OF INTERVENTIONS

The field of education is littered with types of interventions, some very complicated and some relatively simple. The key is to choose one that is appropriate for the specific individual's needs, one that is research based, and one that gets results. This chapter will conclude by detailing one time-tested intervention: tutoring.

A tutor can be any person "undertaking a role to support and enable students to learn" (Cornelius & Higgison, 2000). Research has indicated that tutoring works; many published studies have discovered its positive effects on achievement (Cohen, Kulik, & Kulik, 1982; Topping, 1996; Roscoe & Chi, 2007; Dioso-Henson, 2012).

Tutoring has two main benefits: its ability to adapt to the individual learner's needs and the emotional benefits of the one-on-one relationship (Potter, 1999). Through tutoring, instruction can be conveyed at the student's individual pace or learning style. The tutor can modify learning cues based on one student's response, and simple misunderstandings can be discovered without delay. Tutoring is also emotionally stabilizing in that there is no competition from faster learners. Through brain research, we now know that a student's emotional state strongly affects learning. It is important that the tutor creates a positive learning experience (Shoemaker & Eklund, 1989). In addition, shy or insecure children may find it easier to risk making a mistake in a one-on-one environment.

The concept of peer tutoring has also shown great promise in the classroom. Because children are learning from their peers, they tend to use a similar language, and both parties generally feel more open to expressing their ideas and concerns (Kalkowski, 1995). Research on peer tutoring points out that the intervention is relatively efficient in improving both tutees' and tutors' scholastic and social development, including those with disabilities (Swengel, 1991; Mitchell, 2008).

Students need to feel that tutoring is an opportunity, not a punishment (Schneider, 2000). If students perceive tutoring as a chance to improve themselves, not only will they walk away with extra knowledge of their core classes, but they'll also walk away with improved self-worth and confidence.

Providing interventions to students today can help prevent many social ills in the future. Findings from a recent study identified that students receiving some form of intervention failed fewer classes per year and increased their likelihood of graduation (Cook, 2014). By increasing the chance of graduation, the chance of dropping out decreases. In 1992, almost half of the U.S. prison population were high school dropouts (Ainsworth, 1995). By 2008, 68 percent of state prison inmates did not have a high school diploma (Dropouts and Crime, 2008). An African American male dropout has a 70 percent chance of being imprisoned by the time he is 35 years old (Hamilton Project, 2014). Dropouts are three times more likely to be unemployed than high school graduates. In 2012, almost 50 percent of high school dropouts were not employed (Ansberry, 2012).

Providing the additional time and support to students who need it will increase the chances of them becoming productive adults we will be honored to have taught.

REFLECTION SCENARIO

The leadership team of a school has asked the data coach and math department to sift and sort students according to first-quarter benchmark assessments in Algebra I in order to tier instruction. Most of the students fall into Tier 3, and Tier 2 has more students than Tier 1. What are some strategies that the math department might try to fill in the gaps for their students in the most efficient ways possible? Explain what RTI looks like at your school and describe your role(s) in tiered instruction.

Chapter 15

The Role of Coaching in Education

The beginning of knowledge is the discovery of something we do not understand.

—Frank Herbert

Coaching helps you take stock of where you are now in all aspects of your life, and how that compares to where you would like to be.

—Elaine MacDonald

Professional athletes Stephen Curry and Rory McIlroy, although on top of their sports professions, employ coaches to improve their success rate. Coaches in the field of education also improve success rate. Unfortunately, in many schools, when professional development is provided, no additional support is available. Whether the professional development opportunity is a one-day workshop or an academy offered over several months, the practices and strategies are not likely to be implemented successfully without more support, such as from a coach.

Like professional athletes on top of their game, good teachers and administrators also always strive for improvement. Different studies show that educators are more likely to implement new strategies when they have coaching and feedback accompanying their professional development (Neufeld & Roper, 2003).

In his book *Masterful Coaching*, Robert Hargrove defines a coach as "someone who (1) sees what others may not see through the high quality of his or her attention or listening, (2) is in the position to step back (or invite participants to step back) from the situation so that they have enough distance from it to get some perspective, (3) helps people see the difference between their intentions and their thinking or actions, and (4) helps people cut through patterns of illusion and self-deception caused by defensive thinking and behavior" (Hargrove, 2008).

Published descriptions (Poglinco et al., 2003; Anderson & Anderson, 2004; Bloom, Castagna, Moir, & Warren, 2005) show coaches fulfill a wide range of roles, including the following:

- Help teachers implement new curricular programs
- Consult with and mentor teachers and administrators
- Support educators as they embed knowledge, skills, and techniques into their daily practice
- Plan and research
- Lead discussion groups
- Facilitate study or book groups
- Help teachers think through their teaching practices by trust building with the teacher, listening, observing, questioning, and giving specific feedback.

Per researcher Jim Knight, there are four areas where coaches can work with teachers to get the biggest impact (Knight, 2013):

- *Content planning*: Is the teacher spending adequate time on the most important content?
- *Formative assessment*: Does the teacher know what the learning expectations are, how well each student is achieving them, and what adjustments to instruction should be made based on the student data?
- *Instruction*: Is the classroom instruction effective in increasing student learning?
- *Community building*: Is the teacher creating a positive learning environment?

When effective coaches work with teachers who are open to the experience, teachers get better at their profession.

BENEFITS OF COACHING

Reports have found that significant improvements in student achievement materialized only when site-level guidance and support was provided to the teacher (Joyce & Showers, 1995). When training or professional development is accompanied by coaching, the transfer of material into the classroom increases to 80–90 percent, compared to 5–10 percent without coaching.

Coaching has also been shown to retain teachers. Approximately 50 percent of new teachers leave the profession within five years (Phillips, 2015). One reason teachers begin to lose their commitment to the professional is lack of support or perceived poor working conditions (Kelley, 2004). Because good coaches understand how to partner with other adults and are effective in communicating (listening and speaking), having an academic coach can help teachers feel adequately supported, remain motivated, and limit burn out (Joyce & Showers, 2002; Knight, 2011).

For a coach to assist a teacher, the principal and coach need to know their roles. The principal and coach should meet to clarify their roles and create a transparent relationship. There are eight strategies that can help administrators and coaches collaborate to bring positive change and increased student academic achievement to their school (Moller & Pankake, 2006):

1. *Collaboratively create a plan and monitor the plan regularly.* Do the administrator and the coach have the same vision? Has a timeline been set with long-term and short-term goals? Has time been set aside to meet regularly?
2. *Discuss roles and relationship.* Has the principal stated his/her expectations of the coach, and has the coach stated his/her expectations of the principal? Outlining a clear job description for the coach and making this job description known to the staff can assist in limiting resistance and divisiveness within the staff. The administrator and coach need to have a working relationship, so it is worth the time to discuss when their roles will be the same (observing teachers, analyzing assessments) and when they will differ (evaluation vs. feedback, supervisor vs. peer).
3. *Be available.* Is the principal accessible to the coach for problem solving and discerning the staff's professional needs? Coaches are powerless without the action of the principal. The coach must regularly communicate with the principal regarding the needs of the faculty as well as the successes and challenges being faced.
4. *Provide access to resources.* Does the coach have access to data, materials, and human resources?
5. *Focus on instructional leadership.* Does the role of the coach focus on increasing teacher capacity? The coach should remain an academic asset and not be used for operational tasks such as inventory, discipline, or substitute teaching.
6. *Avoid overload.* Are the coach's responsibilities realistic?
7. *Assist the coach's relationship with peers.* Does the instructional staff know exactly what the coach is expected to do and not do? Has the coach been given low-risk tasks to help ease him/her into the new role? Is the

coach given opportunities to share successes with the staff? The role of both the coach and the principal should be explained to the staff as well as what the expectations are for the "coachees." By showing that they are fully behind the coaching protocol, administrators can eliminate some of the resistance the coach might encounter.

8. *Provide development opportunities.* Has professional development been made available to academic coaches to prepare them for the responsibilities of being a coach?

THE COACH'S ROLES AND RESPONSIBILITIES

A concerted effort to define roles and expectations for the new academic coach will position all for success as administrators, coaches, educators, and staff are united in their goal for a culture of learning and increased student academic achievement at their site.

The teacher-coach relationship is truly a relationship, meaning that it takes time to build and trust needs to be a key factor if it is to succeed. One study found that within six weeks of starting a new school year, 85 percent of teachers who worked with instructional coaches implemented at least one new instructional strategy (Deussen, Coskie, Robinson, & Autio, 2007). When done correctly, coaching involves identifying and acknowledging the teacher's individual strengths, confirming what the teacher was doing correctly, connecting with the teacher's interests, trying to make personal connections with the teacher, and probably asking many questions.

The coach cannot be successful, though, unless the teacher openly gives access to the classroom and is willing to listen to what the coach has to say. The teacher needs to know that the coach is there to help, not to evaluate or "tattle" to the principal about the teacher's weaknesses. As stated in the beginning of this chapter, even the best athletes have coaches to help them get better. This should be no different in the classroom. No matter if the teacher has been in the profession for 30 years or 30 minutes, in a culture of learning the focus should be on continuous improvement.

REFLECTION SCENARIO

Mr. Mathis has just come on board as the new instructional coach at DeGrazia Middle School. He has set up appointments with the staff and schedules an appointment with you next Tuesday morning before school begins. Mr. Mathis starts the meeting by sharing his roles and responsibilities as a coach. He explains that he is here to give feedback to the teachers and assist in helping teachers to move their practices forward. What questions would you have for the new coach? What would you want to know that might help build the trust relationship that research says must exist to foster a successful coaching experience for teachers? Think about the areas of strength and weakness in your own practice. Look back at the coaching strategies in this chapter and describe how a coach might help you to move to the next level in your teaching.

Chapter 16

Professional Development for Teaching and Learning

To keep abreast of this new knowledge and understanding, educators at all levels must be continuous learners throughout the entire span of their professional careers.

—Thomas Guskey

There are no great limits to growth because there are no limits of human intelligence, imagination, and wonder.

—Ronald Reagan

As educators, professional development (PD) is not only a necessary requirement for continuing certification, but also necessary for continuing to grow and improve as a teacher.

Author Thomas Guskey defines professional development as "those processes and activities designed to enhance the professional knowledge, skills, and attitudes of educators so that they in turn, improve the learning of students" (Guskey, 2000). *Staff development, in-service*, and *training* are all terms used interchangeably with professional development (Garet, Porter, Desimone, Birman, & Yoon, 2001).

For professional development to make a difference, it should be continuous, job embedded, data driven, and targeted to the specific needs of students and staff (Fullan, 1991; Reitzug, 2002; Sparks, 2002). Possible data points to analyze and inform professional development need include student-level data, observation data from informal walk-throughs, formal evaluations, peer coaching observations, and teacher reflection journals.

PLANNING FOR INDIVIDUALIZED PROFESSIONAL DEVELOPMENT

There are three key ideas to assist the teacher in planning a successful professional development program (Guskey, 2000):

- First, it is important to have a clear professional goal in mind and determine what outcomes you will expect because of the professional development.
- Second, the goals should be meaningful to the individual teacher.
- Finally, the teacher must decide how he/she will know if the goal is reached and set benchmarks to gauge progress and success along the way.

Delivery methods and platforms for professional development provide opportunities for new learning and have been categorized by several experts into what is known as the seven major models of professional development (Drago-Severson, 1994; Guskey, 2000; Joyce & Showers, 1995, Sparks & Loucks-Horsley, 1989). Figure 16.1 provides a list of the models with the description of how experts define each.

Model	Description
Training	Classic workshop often used to give an overview on a topic or topics to many participants at once
Observation/Assessment	Administrators observe participants or peers who give feedback on their performance, participants' reflections drive change in practice
Improvement Process	Participants are asked to research, develop, and implement a program to bring about reform
Study Groups	Participants study and work together to solve an identified problem
Inquiry/Action Research	Participants improve their classroom practice by conducting action research
Individually Guided Study	Participant identifies an area of focus for personal growth and selects activities and assessments to foster own learning
Mentoring	Less experienced participants are matched with a master educator to develop a mutually beneficial relationship that will lead to a sharing of ideas and growth for both mentor and mentee

Figure 16.1 The Seven Models of Professional Development. Adapted from Guskey, T. R. (2000). *Evaluating professional development*. Thousand Oaks, CA: Corwin Press, Inc.

TEACHER ACTION RESEARCH AS PROFESSIONAL DEVELOPMENT

Teacher action research is the reflective, systematic process identifying a problem and then conducting an inquiry that helps the educator understand more fully the "nature of the problem" (Stringer, 2007). Teacher action research is unique in that, in most cases, it leads to an understanding of the problem particular to that teacher's classroom practice and leads to action particular to that classroom. Teacher action research has four steps (Mills, 2007):

- Identify an area of focus
- Collect data
- Analyze and interpret data
- Develop an action plan

Teacher action research must be a process that teachers determine to undertake of their own volition and not something that they are directed to do (Mills, 2007). This type of professional development is usually selected by unique individuals who are highly committed to continuous improvement and to a culture of learning.

PROFESSIONAL LEARNING COMMUNITIES

Districts and schools that promote a culture of learning encourage a variety of professional development opportunities and provide operational flexibility to ensure planned time and schedules that accommodate educators. One structure that has been shown to be effective for professional development is the professional learning community (PLC). A PLC is "a group of responsible educators who are committed to and share a common purpose of continuous learning. The focus is not only on their own learning but specifically on studying and acquiring whatever it takes to ensure their students are learning" (Hord, 2009). Collaboration has been identified as a key component in professional development and is the foundation of professional learning communities (DuFour, 2004). In recent years, the definition of professional learning communities has become blurred and used in education to signify anything from a book study group to a school department team (DuFour, 2004). Through professional learning communities, members of the school community can purposefully collaborate to learn and construct meaning together with colleagues (DuFour, 2004; Hord, 2009; Vygotsky, 1978).

COACHES

Perhaps one of the most important supports leadership can provide for teachers engaged in professional development is an effective instructional coach. As stated in chapter 15, research has shown that the likelihood of a teacher effectively implementing the new professional development learning in the classroom increases from 5–10 percent without coaching to 80–95 percent with coaching (Joyce & Showers, 2002). It is important to be open to the instructional coach and build a trusting relationship over time. The expectation of the coach is to observe and provide timely and specific feedback to the teachers. Coaches model lessons and may also deliver training and professional development.

One caution needs to be stated clearly at this point. One of the most effective skills an instructional coach must have is the ability to develop trusting relationships (Toll, 2005). Leadership needs to understand that the coach is there to assist the teacher; the coach should not be placed in an evaluative role. It is inappropriate to place the coach in anything other than a coaching relationship with the teachers.

No matter what model of professional development a teacher chooses, the end result should always be to improve teacher knowledge and skills and increase student academic achievement. An effective instructional coach can be a valuable asset to teachers and assist in the implementation of professional development at the practice level.

REFLECTION SCENARIO

Think about where you might see yourself in the education profession in the next three years. What is your professional goal? What are your expected outcomes when you achieve your goals? What will this mean for your practice and your students?

Chapter 17

How to Present Information to Peers

This joy of discovery is real, and it is one of our rewards. So too is the approval of our work by our peers.

—Henry Taube

Live by this credo: have a little laugh at life and look around you for happiness instead of sadness. Laughter has always brought me out of unhappy situations.

—Red Skelton

Research has shown that when teachers work together and learn from each other, they improve their craft by linking research to practice and uniting pedagogical and disciplinary knowledge (NCTE, 2010). Because of the demonstrated benefits, teachers are more often asked to present to their colleagues on professional development days or after returning from a conference. Whether presenting for a large group (all the math teachers in the district) or a small group (a content team), teachers should model best teaching practices for their peers, who are also adult learners. Anita Archer offers a few points about how to present to a large group of adults (Archer, 2007):

- Set the tone. Make participation required but also enjoyable, just as an effective teacher would in the classroom. Participant engagement in staff development equates to the expectation of student engagement when teaching at the classroom level.
- Model each activity to help participants understand what is expected.
- Remember to incorporate wait time. This is important for adults as well.

- Model think/pair/share. Walk the room and write some of the audience responses on an overhead, a paper, or a tablet. Share these responses with the group. Remember, just because they are adults does not mean they do not need to actively participate in their learning.
- Chunk information in the presentation and give participants plenty of time to process the information.
- Continually assess the audience for understanding and provide examples of successful learning. If possible, in addition to a slide presentation, use a document camera or another device that can show participant responses and products that the participants create during presentation activities. Make sure that the participant responses displayed to the whole group are accurate/correct.
- Have high expectations for the audience. High expectations demonstrate respect.
- Get to know the audience. Show up early and talk to participants to find out what they know (background knowledge) and what they are hoping to get out of the presentation.
- Scaffold the skills that are being presented. For example, when Dr. Archer presents to groups of teachers who are not reading specialists, she spends plenty of time on the key parts of reading instruction before addressing strategies. What is *phonemic awareness*? What is *fluency*? What is *decoding*? What is *comprehension*?
- If applicable, make use of participant name tags to be able to call on participants by name.
- Engage the audience with humor and personal stories. Have fun and add levity to your presentation, but make sure that engagement activities and personal stories tie back to the subject matter.
- Wander the room, but stop and stand in one place when talking. Walking and talking at the same time can be distracting.
- State key and crucial information from the same location or spot in the room. This is usually in the front of the room where most of the participants can see the presenter.
- Stick to the parts of the presentation that matter and are applicable to the audience.
- Keep a pace or rhythm in the presentation.

Occasionally, an adult in the audience will be a challenging participant. Maybe someone will ask too many questions or questions that are so specific to his/her circumstances that the answer would not be relevant to anyone else. With these participants, listen to them and never get angry. Look at them as they pose a question, then turn toward the entire audience. Generalize the question and give an answer to the entire group. If it is a personal question, explain that due to time it will need to be addressed after the presentation and then follow up with the individual and address the question as promised.

For planning the design of the presentation, researchers Carl Dunst and Carol Trivette identified certain design practices that will more actively and effectively engage adult learners (Dunst & Trivette, 2012):

- *Introduction*: When introducing the topic, describe key elements, provide examples, and demonstrate application.
- *Application*: Provide time for people to practice. Observe how the participants are applying the new knowledge and provide feedback and guidance.
- *Evaluation/reflection*: Provide the opportunity for the participants to evaluate their use of the new knowledge and reflect upon the experience.
- *Multiple sessions*: If possible, provide multiple opportunities for the participants to repeat what they learned.

Although many best practice strategies used for teaching children are similar for teaching adults, there are a few differences. Following the tips described in this chapter will increase the possibility of creating a great learning experience for peers.

REFLECTION SCENARIO

Think about a time that you attended a professional development in-service or training session. How did the presenter structure the learning? Are there any strategies mentioned in this chapter that the presenter did well? Are there any strategies you would add? Explain the reason why you would choose these specific strategies.

Chapter 18

Some Parting Words from the Authors

When making decisions ask yourself if you are deciding from a place of love or fear. If the answer is fear, do not do it . . . no matter how much easier it is.

—Lori McConaghy Newman

You may encounter many defeats, but you must not be defeated. In fact, it may be necessary to encounter the defeats, so you can know who you are, what you can rise from, how you can still come out of it.

—Maya Angelou

We have spent 17 chapters discussing ways to ensure every teacher is prepared to help every student succeed in school. In closing, we would like to provide a quick cheat sheet of suggestions to keep students motivated in class, some of which have already been introduced within the book and are being emphasized again due to their importance (many of the best practices that have been addressed benefit many different areas within education, including special education; hence, they are called *best practices*).

Suggestion #1: Students who feel their teachers are supportive and care about their success are more engaged in class and have higher success in their learning (Heller, Calderon, & Medrich, 2003; Tkatchov & DeVries, 2017).

Being supportive and building students' confidence is not accomplished by blindly telling them they are doing a great job every day. It involves assessing weaknesses and strengths and delivering feedback in a timely manner so that they can build their skills to complete the task at hand. A good teacher increases the students' *self-efficacy*, the belief that they can and will be successful. Providing specific feedback to students—making the successes and errors transparent and proving suggestions for correcting the errors—increases students' self-efficacy by showing them exactly how they can get better.

Suggestion #2: Avoid overuse of extrinsic rewards, such as candy or toys (Marzano, 1992; Wrzeniewski, 2014).

Extrinsic motivation comes from the outside, such as a materialistic reward. In order for something to be considered a reward, it must be expected and have commercial value (Tileston, 2004). Extrinsically rewarding students for completing work with toys, snacks, and even money can have the unintended consequence of diminishing their desire to learn for learning's sake (Wrzesniewski, 2014). If rewards are used, reward only efforts that truly deserve to be rewarded. Giving a prize for minimal success conveys a message to the student that minimum effort is adequate (Brooks, Freiburger, & Grotheer, 1998). Students who do what they are supposed to do should be acknowledged (with a simple, "Thanks for doing this," or "I see you have your pencil out and are ready to learn. Excellent!"), but simply following instructions is not usually worthy of a reward.

Intrinsic motivation occurs from the inside; we are intrinsically motivated when we have the feeling of self-accomplishment or discovery. Intrinsic motivation has three key parts: autonomy, mastery, and purpose (Pink, 2011). Autonomy basically means the students have freedom to choose; they can make their own decisions. Mastery means they will be getting better at something. Purpose means they are driven to complete the assignment or to learn because they are actually interested in the topic.

Allowing students to have a choice in assignments and input on success/grading criteria is a strategy for addressing all three of the key elements of intrinsic motivation to learn. According to Robert Marzano, "When students are working on goals they themselves have set, they are more motivated . . . and they achieve more than they do when working to meet goals set by the teacher" (Marzano et al., 1992). If a student feels a task is important and the chance of success is high, an increased amount of intrinsic motivation is applied to the task. For the task to be deemed important, it has to satisfy a personal goal or assist in achieving a personal goal.

Suggestion #3: Ensure that classroom expectations for performance and behavior are clearly posted and consistently applied (Skinner & Belmont, 1991; Marzano, 2003).

As previously stated in chapter 2, it is crucial that a teacher explains what is expected, models what is expected, consistently applies consequences for not meeting expectations, and consistently praises when expectations are met.

Suggestion #4: Help students understand the criteria for individual assignments by providing a rubric with detailed grading criteria (Strong, Silver, & Robinson, 1995; Moss & Brookhart, 2009).

Promote mastery learning whenever possible (Anderman & Midgley, 1998). Rubrics, as previously discussed in chapter 13, provide students with the criteria for a certain grade or point range. Rubrics make the assignment expectations clear.

Suggestion #5: Work to build quality relationships with students (McCombs & Pope, 1994; Marzano, 2011).

Taking the time to build relationships with students shows them that you care about them as individuals. Building these one-on-one relationships cannot be stressed enough. Relationships are the building blocks for effective classroom climate and culture.

With at-risk students, try to talk with them individually for two minutes a day for two weeks about any appropriate topic they find interesting. This will help to establish a deeper understanding of an otherwise withdrawn or defensive child's interests and background.

Suggestion #6: Evaluate students based on their own performance on an assignment, not in comparison with the rest of the class (Anderman & Midgley, 1998, Reeves, 2011).

Students should know they are being evaluated based on set criteria, not the teacher's personal preference. The students should clearly understand and see evidence that they are not being judged against their peers, but that they are being evaluated based on their performance of grade-level criteria. This is another reason to use a rubric.

Suggestion #7: Provide students with the chance to respond to questions (Rowe, 1974; Stahl, 1985).

The more students respond to questions and discuss their learning, the more they increase their understanding of skills (Mastropieri & Scruggs, 2000). Use techniques mentioned in chapter 8 for active engagement such as choral response, hand signaling, and partner reading to keep students engaged in the lesson.

THE SUBCUTANEOUS TISSUE STUDENT

As a teacher, no matter what grade level, no matter how hard you try to engage the entire class or implement the suggestions above, you will still encounter "that one kid" who will get under your skin: the class clown, the smartass, the student who acts like you are pulling his/her teeth every time you ask him/her to do something, the kid who always has to say "this is stupid." They are just part of the clientele base we serve and they can drive us to drinking (figuratively speaking . . . and sometimes literally). Please remember that you are the adult. The negativity or resistance "that one kid" radiates can be handled in a way that does not disturb the class structure. Professional educators need to be selective about which battles to fight and when and how to fight them.

If there is a disruptive behavior in the classroom from the class or a specific student, we need to find a way to change that behavior. Screaming, "Stop it!" tends not to work. Researchers recommend the following five steps (Mather & Goldstein, 2001):

1. Define the behavior. Why is it happening? When is it happening? How often does it happen?
2. Design a way to change the behavior. For example: "The student tends to act up after lunch. Maybe if I make sure to include a hands-on activity immediately after lunch, the behavior will stop."
3. Track whether the change is working.
4. Most importantly, praise the new behavior. Once a student is behaving properly, let him/her know: "I see you are at your desk quietly writing in your journal. Thanks."
5. Consistently apply whatever you did that changed the behavior.

As the years go on, issues will come up that you must adapt to, and students will walk through your class who test your patience. Applying the knowledge and skills in this book to your teaching will help you to make the moments you enjoy and the moments when you succeed greatly outnumber the days that require a bottle opener.

We thank you for joining us in this journey. Cheers to a productive school year and many more to come!

Bibliography

Ainsworth, R. G. (1995). *Turning potential school dropouts into graduates: The case for school-based one-on-one tutoring*. (Research Report 95). Washington, DC: National Commission for Employment Policy.

Aghar, G. (2008). The role of school organizational climate in occupational stress among secondary school teachers in Tehran. *International Journal of Occupational Medicine and Environmental Health*, 21(4), 319–329.

Akey, T. M. (2006). *School context, student attitudes and behavior, and academic achievement: An exploratory analysis*. New York: MDRC.

Alexander, K. L., Entwisle, D. R., & Dauber, S. L. (1996). Children in motion: School transfers and elementary school performance. *Journal of Educational Research*, 90(1), 3–12.

Alexander, R. (2010). *Children, their World, their Education. Final Report and Recommendations of the Cambridge Primary Review*. London: Routledge.

Anderman, L. H., & Midgley, C. (1998). *Motivation and middle school students*. Champaign, IL: ERIC Clearinghouse on Elementary and Early Childhood Education.

Anderson, D., & Anderson, M. (2004). *Coaching that counts: Harnessing the power of leadership coaching to deliver strategic value*. Burlington, MA: Elsevier.

Anderson, L., Krathwohl, D., Airasain, P., Cruikshank, K., Mayer, R., Pintrich, O. P., Raths, J., & Wittrock, M. (2001). *A taxonomy for learning, teaching, and assessing*. Addison Wesley.

Andrewes, S. (2003). *Group work v. whole-class activities*. Retrieved from http://www.teachingenglish.org.uk/think/articles/group-work-v-whole-class-activities.

Ansberry, C. (2012). As job market mends, dropouts fall behind. *The Wall Street Journal*

Archer, A. (2007). *Competent students, competent teachers*. Paper presented at the Struggling Adolescents conference in Phoenix, AZ.

Archer, A., & Hughes, C. (2011). *Explicit instruction: Effective and efficient teaching*. New York: Guilford.

Aronson, E., & Patnoe, S. (1997). *The jigsaw classroom: Building cooperation in the classroom* (2nd ed.). New York: Addison Wesley Longman

Achmad, D., & Yusuf, Y. (2014). Observing pair-work task in an English speaking class. *International Journal of Instruction*, 7(1).

Arizona Department of Education. (2017). Arizona academic standards. Retrieved from http://www.azed.gov/standards-practices/k-12-standards-feedback/standards-draft-and-public-comments/.

Armstrong, D. G., Henson, K. T., & Savage, T. (2005). *Teaching today: An introduction to education* (7th ed.). Upper Saddle River, NJ: Pearson Prentice Hall.

Arter, J., & McTighe, J. (2001). *Scoring rubrics in the classroom.* Thousand Oaks, California, Corwin Press.

Bajak, A. (2014). *Lectures aren't just boring, they're ineffective, too, study finds.* Retrieved from http://www.sciencemag.org/news/2014/05/lectures-arent-just-boring-theyre-ineffective-too-study-finds.

Baker, M. L., Sigmon, J. N., & Nugent, M. E. (2001). *Truancy reduction: Keeping students in school.* Washington, DC: U.S. Department of Justice.

Baleni Z. (2015). Online formative assessment in higher education: Its pros and cons. *The Electronic Journal of eLearning*, 13(4), 228–235.

Belot, M., & James, J. (2009). Healthy school meals and educational outcomes. *Journal of Health Economics*, 30(3), 489–504.

Bamburg, J. (1994). *Raising expectations to improve student learning.* Oak Brook, Illinois: North Central Regional Educational Laboratory,

Bandura, A. (1997). *Self-efficacy: The exercise of control.* New York: W.H. Freeman.

Beck, I. L., McKeown, M. G., & Kucan, L. (2003). Taking delight in words: Using oral language to build young children's vocabularies. *American Educator*, 27(1).

Belland, B., Glazewski, K, & Richardson, J. (2008). A scaffolding framework to support the construction of evidence-based arguments among middle school students. *Education Technology Research and Development*, 56(4), 401–422.

Ben-Sasson, A., Carter A., & Briggs-Gowan, M. (2009). Sensory over-responsivity in elementary school: Prevalence and social-emotional correlates. *Journal of Abnormal Child Psychology*, 37(5).

Berla, N., Henderson, A. T., & Kerewsky, W. (1989). *The middle school years: A parent's handbook.* Columbia, MD: National Committee for Citizens in Education.

Bernhardt, V. (2004). *Data analysis for continuous school improvement* (2nd ed.). Larchmont, NY: Eye on Education.

Black, P. J., & Wiliam, D. (1998). Inside the black box. Raising standards through classroom assessment. *Phi Delta Kappan*, 80, 139–148.

Black, S. (2007). Achievement by design. *American School Board Journal*, 194(10), 39–41.

Blank, W. (1997). Authentic instruction. In W. E. Blank & S. Harwell (Eds.), *Promising practices for connecting high school to the real world*, 15–21. Tampa, FL: University of South Florida.

Blatchford, P., Hallam, S., Kutnick, P., & Creech, A. (2008). *Classes, groups and transitions: Structures for teaching and learning. Primary review research survey 9/2.* Cambridge: University of Cambridge.

Bloom, G., Castagna, C., Moir, E., & Warren, B. (2005). *Blended coaching: Skills and strategies to support principal development.* Thousand Oaks, CA: Corwin Press.

Blumer, H. (1969). *Symbolic interactionism: Perspective and method.* Englewood Cliffs, NJ: Prentice-Hall.

Boaler, J. (2013). Ability and mathematics: The mindset revolution that is reshaping education. *Forum,* 55(1), 143–152.

Bond, L. (1996). Norm- and criterion-referenced testing. *Practical Assessment, Research & Evaluation,* 5(2).

Bonk, C. J., & Graham, C. R. (2006). *Handbook of blended learning: Global perspectives, local designs.* San Francisco, CA: Pfeiffer Publishing.

Bonus, M., & Riordan, L. (1998). *Increasing student on-task behavior through the use of specific seating arrangements.* Unpublished master's thesis, Saint Xavier University, Chicago, IL.

Bonwell, C. C., & Eison, J. A. (1991). *Active learning: Creating excitement in the classroom.* Washington, DC: *ASHE-ERIC Higher Education Report No. 1.*

Bransford, J., Brown, A. L., Cocking, R. R., & National Research Council (1999). *How people learn: Brain, mind, experience, and school.* Washington, DC: National Academy Press.

Brewster, C., & Fager, J. (2000). *Increasing student engagement and motivation: From time-on-task to homework.* Portland, OR: Northwest Regional Educational Laboratory.

Brooks, S. R., Freiburger, S. M., & Grotheer, D. R. (1998). *Improving elementary student engagement in the learning process through integrated thematic instruction.* Unpublished master's thesis, Saint Xavier University, Chicago, IL.

Brookhart, M. S. (2010). *How to assess higher-order thinking skills in your classroom.* Alexandria, VA: Association of Supervision and Curriculum Development.

Burton, K. (2015). Continuing my journey on designing and refining criterion-referenced assessment rubrics. *Journal of Learning Design,* 8(3).

Chall, J. S. (1983). *Stages of reading development.* New York: McGraw-Hill.

Chall, J. S., Jacobs, V. A., & Baldwin, L. E. (1990). *The reading crisis: Why poor children fall behind.* Cambridge, MA: Harvard University Press.

Chang, Y. S., Labovitz, G., & Rosansky, V. (1992). *Making quality work: A leadership guide for the results-driven manager.* Essex Junction, VT: Omneo.

Chapman, C., & King, R.(2003). *Differentiated instructional strategies for reading in the content areas.* Thousand Oaks, CA: Corwin Press, Inc.

Chapman, E. (2003). Alternative approaches to assessing student engagement rates. *Practical Assessment, Research & Evaluation,* 8(13).

Chappuis, S., Commodore, C., & Stiggins, R. (2017). *Balanced assessment systems: Leadership, quality, and the role of classroom assessment.* Thousand Oaks, CA: Corwin Press, Inc., 28–29.

Chenoweth, K. (2014). Curriculum vs. Standards in the Common Core Debate. Retrieved from The Education Trust website: https://edtrust.org/the-equity-line/distinguishing-standards-curriculum/.

Chigeza, P., & Halbert, K. (2014). Navigating e-learning and blended learning for pre-service teachers: Redesigning for engagement, access and efficiency. *Australian Journal of Teacher Education,* 39(11).

Christen, W. L., & Murphy T. J. (1991). Increasing comprehension by activating prior knowledge. *ERIC Digest*. Bloomington, IN: *ERIC Clearinghouse on Reading, English, and Communication.*

Christle, C. A., Jolivette, K., & Nelson, C. M. (2007). School characteristics related to high school dropout rates. *Remedial and Special Education*, 28(6), 325–339.

Cohen, P.A., Kulik, J.A., & Kulik, C. L. C. (1982). Educational outcomes of tutoring: A meta-analysis of findings. *American Educational Research Journal*, 19, 237–248.

Cook, P., Dodge, K., Farkas, G., Fryer, Jr, R. G., Guryan, J., Ludwig, J., Mayer, S., Pollack, H., & Steinberg, L. (2014). *The (surprising) efficacy of academic and behavioral intervention with disadvantaged youth: Results from a randomized experiment in Chicago*. National Bureau of Economic Research, Working Papers. No. 19862.

Conrad, D. (2005). Building and maintaining community in cohort based online learning. *Journal of Distance Education*, 20(1), 1–20.

Cornelius, S., & Higgison, C. (2000). *The tutor's role. Online Tutoring E-book.*

Cotton, K. (1989). *Classroom questioning. Close Up #5*. Portland, OR: Northwest Regional Educational Laboratory.

———. (2001). *Expectations and student outcomes*. Retrieved from http://education-northwest.org/sites/default/files/ExpectationsandStudentOutcomes.pdf.

Cunningham, A. E., & Stanovich, K. E. (1997). Early reading acquisition and its relation to reading experience and ability 10 years later. *Developmental Psychology*, 33, 934–945.

Darling-Hammond, L., & McLaughlin, M. W. (1995). Policies that support professional development in an era of reform. *Phi Delta Kappan*, 76 (8), 597–604.

Darling-Hammond, L. (1996). *The role of teacher expertise and experience in students' opportunity to learn. Strategies for linking school finance and students' opportunity to learn.* Washington, DC: National Governors Association.

———. (2000). How teacher education matters. *Journal of Teacher Education*, 51, 166–173.

Darling-Hammond, L., Berry, B., & Thoreson, A. (2001). Does teacher certification matter? Evaluating the evidence. *Educational Evaluation and Policy Analysis*, 23, 57–77.

Dary, T., Pickeral, T., Shumer, R., & Williams, A. (2016). *Weaving student engagement into the core practices of schools: A National Dropout Prevention Center/Network position paper*. Clemson, SC: National Dropout Prevention Center/Network. Retrieved from http://dropoutprevention.org/wp-content/uploads/2016/09/student-engagement-2016-09.pdf.

Davis, S. J., & Winek, J. (1989). Improving expository writing by increasing background knowledge. *Journal of Reading.*

Dean, D. (2008). Sentence combining: Building skills through reading and writing. *Classroom Notes Plus*. Retrieved from http://www.ncte.org/library/NCTEFiles/Resources/Journals/CNP/0261-august08/NP0261Sentence.pdf.

Deci, E. L., Vallerand, R. J., Pelletier, L. G., & Ryan, R. M. (1991). Motivation and education: The self-determination perspective. *Educational Psychologist*, 26(3–4), 325–346.

DeCoste, D. (2014). *The DeCoste writing protocol: Evidence-based research to make instructional and accommodation decisions.* Volo, IL: Don Johnston, Inc.

Department of Education, Science, and Training (2001). *National Report to Parliament on Indigenous Education and Training, Department of Education, Science and Training.* Commonwealth of Australia.

Deussen, T., Coskie, T., Robinson, L., & Autio, E. (2007). *Coach can mean many things: Five categories of literacy coaches in Reading First.* Washington, DC: U.S. Department of Education, Institute of Education Sciences, National Center for Education Evaluation and Regional Assistance, Regional Educational Laboratory Northwest.

Dev, P. (1997). Intrinsic motivation and academic achievement: What does their relationship imply for the classroom teacher? *Remedial and Special Education*, 18(1), 12–19.

DeVries, M., & Tkatchov, O. (2017). Improving outcomes for students with disabilities: Identifying characteristics of successful districts. *Journal of the American Academy of Special Education Professionals,* Winter 2017.

Dioso-Henson, L. (2012). The effect of reciprocal peer tutoring and non-reciprocal peer tutoring on the performance of students in college physics. *Research in Education,* 87, 34–49.

Dochy, F. J. R. C., Segers, M., & Buehl, M. M. (1999). The relation between assessment practices and outcomes of studies: The case of research on prior knowledge. *Review of Educational Research,* 69(2).

Drago-Severson, E. (1994). *What does staff development develop? How the staff development literature conceives adult growth.* Unpublished qualifying paper, Harvard University.

Droop, M., & Verhoeven, L. (2003). Language proficiency and reading ability in first and second language learners. *Reading Research Quarterly,* 38(1).

Drubach, D. (2000). *The brain explained.* Upper Saddle River, NJ: Prentice-Hall, Inc.

Drucker, P. (1992). *Managing for the future: The 1990s and beyond.* New York: Truman Talley Books.

DuFour, R. (2004). What is a "Professional Learning Community?" *Educational Leadership,* 61(8), 6.

Dulewicz, V., Malcolm Higgs, M., Mark Slaski, M. (2003). Measuring emotional intelligence: content, construct and criterion-related validity. *Journal of Managerial Psychology,* 18(5), 405–420.

Dunn, M., Bonner, B., & Huske, L. (2007). *Developing a systems process for improving instruction in vocabulary: Lessons learned.* Alexandria, VA: Association of Supervision and Curriculum Development.

Dunst, C., & Trivette, C. (2012). Moderators of the effectiveness of adult learning method practices. *Journal of Social Sciences,* 8, 143–148.

Dweck, C. (2006). Is math a gift? Beliefs that put females at risk. In S. J. Ceci & W. Williams (Eds.), *Why aren't more women in science? Top researchers debate the evidence.* Washington, DC: American Psychological Association.

———. (2015). Carol Dweck revisits the 'growth mindset. *Education Week,* 35(5).

Echevarria, J., Vogt, M. E., & Short, D. (2004). *Making content comprehensible for English language learners: The SIOP model* (2nd ed.). Boston: Allyn & Bacon.

Eiszler, C. F. (1983). Perceptual preferences as an aspect of adolescent learning styles. *Education,* 103(3), 231–242.

Ellis, N., & Beaton, A. (1993). Factors affecting the learning of foreign language vocabulary: Imagery keyword mediators and phonological short-term memory. *The Quarterly journal of Experimental Psychology,* 46A(3), 533–558.

Englert, C. S. (2009). Connecting the dots in a research program to develop, implement, and evaluate strategic literacy interventions for struggling readers and writers. *Learning Disabilities Research & Practice,* 24(2), 104–120.

Epstein, J. L. (1987). Toward a theory of family-school connections: Teacher practices and parent involvement. In K. Hurrelmann, F. Kaufmann, & F. Losel (Eds.), *Social intervention: Potential and constraints,* 121–136. New York: Aldine.

Evertson, C., & Harris, A. (1992). What we know about managing classrooms. *Educational Leadership,* 49(7), 74–78.

Evertson, C., & Poole, I. (2006). *Effective room arrangement.* Peabody College/ Vanderbilt University Iris Center.

Evertson, C. M., Emmer, E. T., & Worsham, M. E. (2003). *Classroom management for elementary teachers* (6th ed.). Boston, MA: Allyn & Bacon.

Fay, D., & Cutler, A. (1977). Malapropisms and the structure of the mental lexicon. *Linguistic Inquiry,* 8, 505–520.

Ferguson, R. F., & Womack, S. T. (1993). The impact of subject matter and education coursework on teaching performance. *Journal of Teacher Education,* 44(1), 55–63.

Felch, J., Song, J., & Smith, D. (2010). Who's teaching L.A.'s kids? *Los Angeles Times.*

Festus, A., & Kurumeh, M. (2015). Curriculum planning and development in mathematics from the formative stages. *Journal of Education and Practice,* 6, 62–66.

Fetler, M. (1999). High school staff characteristics and mathematics test results. *Education Policy Analysis Archives,* 7(9).

Finn, J. D. (1989). Withdrawing from School. *Review of Educational Research,* 59, 117–142.

Fitterer, H., Harwood, S., Locklear, K., Wright, K., Fleming, P., & Levinsohn, J. (2004). *T4S Classroom Observation Protocol.* WestEd.

Fong, A. B., Bae, S., & Huang, M. (2010). Patterns of student mobility among English language learner students in Arizona public schools. In *Issues & Answers Report, REL 2010–No. 093.* Washington, DC: U.S. Department of Education, Institute of Education Sciences, National Center for Education Evaluation and Regional Assistance, Regional Educational Laboratory West. Retrieved from http://ies.ed.gov/ncee/edlabs.

Forster, M., & Masters, G. (2004). Bridging the conceptual gap between classroom assessment and system accountability. In M. Wilson (Ed.), *Towards coherence between classroom assessment and accountability: The 103rd yearbook of the National Society for the Study of Education, Part II,* 51–73. Chicago: The University of Chicago Press.

Fox, C., Snow, P., & Holland, K. (2014). The relationship between sensory processing difficulties and behaviour in children aged 5–9 who are at risk of developing conduct disorder. *Emotional and Behavioural Difficulties,* 19(1), 71–88.

Francis, E. (2016). *Now THAT'S a good question! How to promote cognitive rigor through classroom questioning.* Alexandria, VA: ASCD.

Frayer, D. A., Frederick,W. D., & Klausmeier, H. J. (1969). *A schema for testing the level of cognitive mastery* (Working Paper No. 16) Madison: Wisconsin Research and Development Center for Cognitive Learning.

Fuchs, D., & Fuchs, L. S. (2005). Responsiveness-to-intervention: A blueprint for practitioners, policymakers, and parents. *Teaching Exceptional Children,* 38, 57–61.

Fullan, M. G. (1991). *The new meaning of educational change.* New York: Teachers College Press.

Fuller, T. (2013). Authentic learning series: 15 classroom literacy ideas for early childhood. (blog post). Retrieved from https://www.nwea.org/blog/2013/authentic-learning-classroom-literacy-ideas-early-childhood/.

Gallagher, K. (2017). The writing journey. *Educational Leadership,* 74(5), 24–29.

Garan, E. M., & DeVoogd, G. (2008). The benefits of sustained silent reading: Scientific research and common sense converge. *The Reading Teacher,* 62(4), 336–344.

Gardner, H., & Hatch, T. (1989). Multiple intelligences go to school: Educational implications of the theory of multiple intelligences. *Educational Researcher,* 18(8), 4–9.

Garet, M., Porter, A., Desimone, L., Birman, B., & Yoon, K. (2001). What makes professional development effective? Results from a national sample of teachers. *American Educational Research Journal,* 38(4), 915–945.

Gaston, A., Martinez, J., & Martin, E. (2016). Embedding literacy strategies in social studies for eighth-grade students. *Journal of Social Studies Education Research,* 7(1), 73–95.

Gasaymeh, A-H. (2011). *The implications of constructivism for rubric design and use.* Higher Education International Conference (HEIC 2011).

Godwin, K. E., Almeda, M. V., Petroccia, M., Baker, R. S., & Fisher, A. V. (2013). Classroom activities and off-task behavior in elementary school children. In M. Knauff, M. Pauen, N. Sebanz, & I. Wachsmuth (Eds.), *Proceedings of the 35th Annual Meeting of the Cognitive Science Society,* 2428–2433.

Gonder, P. (1991). Caught in the middle: How to unleash the potential of average students. Arlington, Virginia: *American Association of School Administrators.*

Good, R. (2011). Formative use of assessment information: It's a process, so let's say what we mean. *Practical Assessment, Research & Evaluation,* 16(3).

Good, T. L. (1987). Two decades of research on teacher expectations: Findings and future directions. *Journal of Teacher Education,* 38(4), 32–47. EJ 358 702.

Gottfredson, D., & Gottfredson, G. (2002). Quality of school-based prevention programs: Results from a National Survey. *Journal of Research in Crime and Delinquency,* 39, 3–35.

Graham, S., & Perin, D. (2007). *Writing next: Effective strategies to improve writing of adolescents in middle and high schools – A report to Carnegie Corporation of New York.* Washington, DC: Alliance for Excellent Education.

Green, M. F. (1989). *Minorities on campus: A handbook for enriching diversity.* Washington, DC: American Council on Education.

Guskey, T. R. (1982). The effects of change in instructional effectiveness on the relationship of teacher expectations and student achievement. *Journal of Educational Research,* 75, 345–349.

———. (2000). Grading policies that work against standards . . . and how to fix them. *NASSP Bulletin,* 84(620), 20–29.

———. (2000). *Evaluating professional development.* Thousand Oaks, CA: Corwin Press, Inc.

———. (2003). How classroom assessments improve learning. *Educational Leadership,* 60(5), 6–11.

Guthrie, J. T., & Humenick, N. M. (2004). Motivating students to read: Evidence for classroom practices that increase reading motivation and achievement. In. P. McCardle & V. Chhabra (Eds.), *The voice of evidence in reading research,* 329–354. Baltimore: Brookes Publishing.

Guthrie, J. T. (2008). *Engaging adolescents in reading.* Thousand Oaks, CA: Corwin Press.

Haberman, M. (1995). Selecting "star" teachers for children and youth in urban poverty. *Phi Delta Kappan,* 76.

Hall, P., & Simeral, A. (2008). *Building teachers' capacity for success: A collaborative approach for coaches and school leaders.* Alexandria: Association for Supervision and Curriculum Development.

Hall, R. M., & Sandler, B. R. (1982). *The classroom climate: A chilly one for women?* Washington, DC: Association of American Colleges,

Hall, S. L. (2008). *Implementing response to intervention: A principal's guide.* Thousand Oaks, CA: Corwin Press.

Hamlin, C. (2011). The writing process: Step-by-step approach curbs plagiarism, helps students build confidence in their writing ability. *Faculty Focus.* Retrieved from https://www.facultyfocus.com/articles/effective-teaching-strategies/the-writing-process-step-by-step-approach-curbs-plagiarism-helps-students-build-confidence-in-their-writing-abilities/

Hanson, K., & Stipek, D. (2014). Schools v. prisons: Education's the way to cut prison population. *Mercury News.* Retrieved from https://ed.stanford.edu/in-the-media/schools-v-prisons-educations-way-cut-prison-population-op-ed-deborah-stipek.

Hanushek, E. (2009). Teacher deselection. In Dan Goldhaber and Jane Hannaway (Eds.), *Creating a new teaching profession.* Washington: Urban Institute Press.

Hargrove, R. (2003). *Masterful coaching.* San Francisco: Jossey-Bass.

Harlacher, J. E., Sanford, A. K., & Nelson, N. J. (2014). *Distinguishing between Tier 2 and Tier 3 instruction in order to support implementation of RTI.* RTI Action Network Monthly Newsletter. Retrieved from http://rtinetwork.org.

Harris, K., Udry, J., Muller, C., & Reyes, P. (2010). *National Longitudinal Study of Adolescent Health, 1994–2008*: Education Data.

Hart, B., & Risley, R. T. (1995). *Meaningful differences in the everyday experience of young American children.* Baltimore: Paul H. Brookes.

Hattie, J. (2012). *Visible learning: A synthesis of over 800 meta-analyses relating to achievement.* New York: Routledge.

Hatzivassiloglou, V., & McKeown, K (1993). *Towards the automatic identification of adjectival scales: Clustering adjectives according to meaning.* ACL 172–182.

Hawk, P., Coble, C. R., & Swanson, M. (1985). Certification: It does matter. *Journal of Teacher Education*, 36(3), 13–15.

Heacox, D. (2002). *Differentiating instruction in the regular classroom: How to reach and teach all learners, grades 3–12.* Minneapolis, MN: Free Spirit.

Heller, R., Calderon, S., & Medrich, E. (2003). *Academic achievement in the middle grades: What does research tell us? A review of the literature.* Atlanta, GA: Southern Regional Education Board.

Heritage, M. (2010). *Formative assessment and next-generation assessment systems: Are we losing an opportunity?* The Council of Chief State School Officers (CCSSO).

———. (2010). *Formative assessment: Making it happen in the classroom.* Thousand Oaks, CA: Corwin Press.

———. (2012). Power Point presentation in Arizona Department of Education formative assessment professional development series webinar, delivered April 2, 2012.

Heritage, M., Kim, J., Vendlinski, T., & Herman, J. (2009). From evidence to action: A seamless process in formative assessment? *Educational Measurement: Issues and Practice*, 28(3), 24–31.

Herzfeldt-Kamprath, R., & Ullrich, R. (2016). *Examining teacher effectiveness between preschool and third grade.* Washington, DC: Center for American Progress.

Honzay, A. (1986). More is not necessarily better. *Educational Research Quarterly*, 11, 2–6

Hord, S. (2009). Professional learning communities: Educators working together toward a shared purpose-improved student learning. *Journal of Staff Development*, 30 (1).

Huey, E., & Swinehart, C. (2015). Applying imagery to vocabulary instruction. *Perspectives of Language and Literacy*, 41(3).

Hunter, D. (2014). A foundation for positive school culture. *ASCDExpress.* Retrieved from http://www.ascd.org/ascd-express/vol9/910-hunter.aspx

Hurst, S. (2014). *What is the difference between RTI and MTSS?* Retrieved from http://www.readinghorizons.com/blog/what-is-the-difference-between-RtI-and-mtss

Jackson, A. W. & Davis, G. A. (2000). *Turning points 2000: Educating adolescents in the 21st century.* New York: Teachers College Press.

Jesse, D. (1995). *Increasing parental involvement: A key to student achievement. What's noteworthy on learners, learning & schooling.* McRel, Mid-Continent Regional Educational Laboratory.

Jones, F. (2000). *Tools for teaching: Discipline, instruction, motivation*, Hong Kong: Fred Jones & Associates, Inc.

———. (2007). *Fred Jones tools for teaching: Discipline, instruction, motivation.* Santa Cruz, CA: Frederic H. Jones and Associates.

Joyce, B., & Showers, B. (1995). *Student achievement through staff development* (2nd ed.). New York: Longman.

———. (2002). *Student achievement through staff development.* Alexandria, VA: Association for Supervision and Curriculum Development.

Joyce, B., Wolf, J., & Calhoun, E. (1993). *The self-renewing school.* Alexandria, VA: Association for Supervision and Curriculum Development.

Kalkowski, P. (1995). Peer and cross-age tutoring. In *School improvement research series; Close-up #18.* Portland, OR: Northwest Regional Educational Laboratory.

Kearney, M., Harris, B., Jácome, E., & Parker, L. (2014). *Ten economic facts about crime and incarceration in the United States.* Washington, DC: Brookings Institution.

Keeler, C. (2013). Writing strategies for struggling writers. *Education Masters.* Paper 246.

Kellough, R., & Kellough, N. (1999). *Secondary school teaching: A guide to methods and resources; Planning for competence.* Upper Saddle River, New Jersey: Prentice Hall.

Kelley, L. M. (2004). Why induction matters. *Journal of Teacher Education,* 55(5), 438.

Ketterlin-Geller, L., & Johnstone, C. (2006). *Accommodations and universal design: Supporting access to assessments in higher education. Journal of Postsecondary Education and Disability,* 19(2).

Kingore, B. (2006). Tiered instruction: Beginning the process. *Teaching for High Potential,* 5–6. www.nagc.org.

Kinne, L. J., Hasenbank, J. F., & Coffey, D. (2014). Are we there yet? Using rubrics to support progress toward proficiency and model formative assessment. *AILACTE Journal,* 11(1), 109–128.

Klein, P. D. (1997). Multiplying the problems of intelligence by eight: A critique of Gardner's theory. *Canadian Journal of Education / Revue canadienne de l'éducation,* 22(4), 377–394.

———. (2011). What good coaches do. *Educational Leadership,* 69, 18–22.

Knight, J. (2013). *High-impact instruction: A framework for great teaching.* Thousand Oaks, CA: Corwin Press.

Kokkinos, C. (2007). Job stressors, personality and burnout in primary school teachers. *British Journal of Educational Psychology,* 77, 229–243.

Kucer, S. (2009). *Dimensions of literacy: A conceptual base for teaching reading and writing in school settings* (3rd ed.). Mahwah, NJ: Erlbaum.

Kushman, J. W., Sieber, C., & Harold-Kinney, P. (2000). This isn't the place for me: School dropout. In D. Capuzzi & D. R. Gross (Eds.), *Youth at risk: A prevention resource for counselors, teachers, and parents* (3rd ed.), 471–507. Alexandria, VA: American Counseling Association.

Laczko-Kerr, I., & Berliner, D. (2002). The effectiveness of teach for America and other under-certified teachers on student academic achievement: A case of harmful public policy. *Educational Policy Analysis Archives,* 10(37).

Langer, J. A., & Applebee, A. N. (1987). *How writing shapes thinking.* Urbana, IL: National Council of Teachers of English.

———. (1984). Examining background knowledge and text comprehension. *Reading Research Quarterly,* 19(4).

Langer, J. A. (2001). Beating the odds: Teaching middle and high school students to read and write well. *American Educational Research Journal,* 38, 837–880.

Lavay, B., French, R., & Henderson, H., (2007). A practical plan for managing the behavior of students with disabilities in general physical education. *Journal of Physical Education, Recreation & Dance,* 78, 42–48.

Learning Point Associates. (2004). *Guide to using data in school improvement efforts: A compilation of knowledge from data retreats and data use at learning point associates.* Learning Point Associates.

Lee, V. E., & Smith, J. B. (1999). Social support and achievement for young adolescents in Chicago: The role of school academic press. *American Educational Research Journal,* 36, 907–945.

Li, J., & O'Connell, A. A. (2012). Obesity, high-calorie food intake, and academic achievement trends among U.S. school children. *The Journal of Educational Research,* 105(6), 391–403.

Linchevski, L., & Kutscher, B. (1998). Tell me with whom you're learning and I'll tell you how much you've learned: Mixed-ability versus same-ability grouping in mathematics. *Journal for Research in Mathematics Education,* 29, 533–554.

Linquanti, R. (2014). *Supporting formative assessment for deeper learning: A primer for policymakers.* Paper prepared for the Formative Assessment for Students and Teachers/State Collaborative on Assessment and Student Standards, 2. Washington, DC: Council of Chief State School Officers.

Lenhart, A., Pew Research Center, (2015). *Teen, social media and technology overview 2015.*

Lent, R. C. (2012). *Overcoming textbook fatigue: 21st century tools to revitalize teaching and learning.* Alexandria, VA: ASCD.

Lipton, L., Wellman, B., & Humbard, C. (2001). *Mentoring matters: A practical guide to learning-focused relationships.* Sherman CT: Miravia.

Long, S. A., Winograd, P. N., & Bridget, C. A. (1989). The effects of reader and text characteristics on imagery reported during and after reading. *Reading Research Quarterly,* 24(3).

Lorenz, B., Green, B., & Brown, A. (2009). Using multimedia graphic organizer software in the prewriting activities of primary school students: What are the benefits? *Computers In the Schools,* 26, 115–119.

Lumsden, L. S. (1994). *Student motivation to learn* (ERIC Digest No. 92). Eugene, OR: ERIC Clearinghouse on Educational Management.

Lyon, G. R. (1997). *Report on learning disabilities research.* Congressional testimony.

MacNeil, A., & Maclin, V. (2005). *Building a learning community: The culture and climate of schools.* Retrieved from the Connexions website: http://cnx.org/content/m12922/1.2/.

Mandel, S. M. (1999). *Virtual field trips in the cyberage: A content mapping approach.* Arlington Heights, IL: SkyLight Professional Development.

Martella, R., Nelson, J., & Marchand-Martella, N. (2003). *Managing disruptive behaviors in the schools.* Boston: Pearson Education.

Marx, A., Fuhrer, U., & Hartig, T. (2000). Effects of classroom seating arrangements on children's question-asking. *Learning Environment Research,* 2, 249–263.

Marzano, R. J., & Pickering D. J. (2005). *Building academic vocabulary: Teacher's manual.* Alexandria, VA: Association for Supervision and Curriculum Development.

Marzano, R. J. (1992). *A different kind of classroom: Teaching with dimensions of learning.* Alexandria, VA: Association for Supervision and Curriculum Development.

Marzano, R. J., Pickering, D. J., Arredondo, D. E., Blackburn, G. J., Brandt, R. S., & Moffett, C. A. (1992). *Dimensions of learning: Training and implementation manual.* Alexandria, VA: Association for Supervision and Curriculum Development.

Marzano, R., Marzano, J., & Pickering, D. (2003). *Classroom management that works.* Alexandria, VA: Association for Supervision and Curriculum Development.

Marzano, R., Walters, T., & McNulty, B. (2005). *School leadership that works.* Alexandria, VA: Association for Supervision and Curriculum Development.

Marzano, R. J. (2004). *Building background knowledge for academic achievement: Research on what works in schools.* Alexandria, VA: Association for Supervision and Curriculum Development.

Mastropieri, M., & Scruggs, T. (2000). *The inclusive classroom: Strategies for effective instruction.* Columbus, OH: Merrill.

Mastrorilli, T. (2016). Understanding the high school dropout process through student engagement and school processes: Evidence from the educational longitudinal study of 2002. *CUNY Academic Works.*

Mather, N., & Goldstein, S. (2001). Behavior modification in the classroom. In *Learning Disabilities and Challenging Behaviors: A Guide to Intervention and Classroom* Management, 96–117.

McCarthy, J., & Still, S. (1993). Hollibrook accelerated elementary school. In J. Murphy & P. Hallinger (Eds.), *Restructuring schooling: Learning from ongoing efforts*, 63–83. Newbury Park, CA: Corwin.

McCombs, B. L., & Pope, J. E. (1994). *Motivating hard to reach students.* Washington, DC: American Psychological Association.

McDiarmid, G. W., David, J. L., Kannapel, P. K., Corcoran, T. B., & Coe, P. (1997). *Professional development under KERA: Meeting the challenge.* Preliminary research findings prepared for The Partnership for Kentucky Schools and The Pritchard Committee for Academic Excellence.

McGreal, S. (2013). The illusory theory of multiple intelligences. *Psychology Today.* Retrieved from https://www.psychologytoday.com/blog/unique-everybody-else/201311/the-illusory-theory-multiple-intelligences.

McInerney, M., & Elledge, A. (2013). *Using a response to intervention framework to improve student learning: A pocket guide for state and district leaders.* Washington, DC: American Institutes for Research.

McKeachie, W., Pintrich, P., Yi-Guang, L., & Smith, D. (1986). *Teaching and learning in the college classroom: A review of the research literature.* Ann Arbor, MI: The Regents of the University of Michigan.

McKenna, M. C., Kear, D. J., & Ellsworth, R. A. (1995). Children's attitudes toward reading: A national survey. *Reading Research Quarterly*, 30, 934–956.

McMillan, J. H. (2000). *Classroom assessment: Principles and practice for effective instruction.* Pearson Technology Group.

Meier, D. (2000). *The accelerated learning handbook: A creative guide to designing and delivering faster, more effective training programs.* McGraw-Hill Professional.

Meiers, M., & Trevitt, J. (2010). Language in the mathematics classroom. *The Digest, NSWIT*, 2010 (2). Retrieved from http://www.nswteachers.nsw.edu.au

Mitchell. D. (2008). *What really works in special and inclusive education: Using evidence-based teaching strategies.* Abingdon, Oxon: Routledge.

Moir, E. (1999). The stages of a teacher's first year. In M. Scherer (Ed.), *A better beginning: Supporting and mentoring new teachers.*

Moller, G., & Pankake, A. (2006). *Lead with me: A principal's guide to teacher leadership.* Larchmont, NY: Eye on Education.

Moss, C. M., & Brookhart, S. M. (2009). *Advancing formative assessment in every classroom: A guide for instructional leaders.* Alexandria, VA: Association for Supervision and Curriculum Development.

Murphy, J. M., Wehler, C. A., Pagano, M. E., Little, M., Kleinman, R. E., & Jellinek, M. S. (1998). Relationship between hunger and psychosocial functioning in low-income American children. *Journal of the American Academy of Child and Adolescent Psychiatry.*

National Assessment of Educational Progress (2015). Average mathematics score lower and reading score unchanged. *The Nation's Report Card.* Retrieved from http://www.nationsreportcard.gov/reading_math_g12_2015/.

National Center for Education Statistics (2005). Integrated postsecondary education data system (IPEDS) fall enrollment survey. Washington, DC U.S. Department of Education.

National Council of Teachers of English (2010). Teacher learning communities. Urbana, IL: Retrieved from http://www.ncte.org/library/NCTEFiles/Resources/Journals/ CC/0202-nov2010/CC0202Policy.pdf

National Research Council (U.S.). Committee on Learning Research and Educational Practice., Bransford, J., Pellegrino, J. W., & Donovan, S. (1999). *How people learn: Bridging research and practice.* Washington, DC: National Academy Press.

National Survey of Student Engagement (2013). Retrieved from http://nsse.iub.edu/.

Neufeld, B., & Roper, D. (2003). *Coaching: A strategy for developing instructional capacity—promises & practicalities.* Washington, DC: Aspen Institute Program on Education and the Annenberg Institute for School Reform.

Northwest Regional Educational Laboratory (1999). *So that every child can read . . . America reads community tutoring partnerships.* Washington, DC: U.S. Department of Education.

Palincsar, A. S., Brown, A. L., & Campione, J. C. (1993). First grade dialogues for knowledge acquisition and use. In E. A. Forman, N. Minick, & C. A. Stone (Eds.), *Contexts for learning: Sociocultural dynamics in children's development,* 43–57. New York: Oxford University Press.

Painter, D. (2016). The computer-based writing program: A clinical teaching experience for education interns to develop professional knowledge and skills in effective instructional writing practices. *Teacher Educators' Journal, 9,* 112–135.

Pemberton, G. (1988). *On teaching minority students: Problems and strategies.* Brunswick, Maine: Bowdoin College.

Penner, J. G. (1984). *Why many college teachers cannot lecture.* Springfield, Ill.

Perie, M., Marion, S., & Gong, B. (2009). Moving toward a comprehensive assessment system: A framework for considering interim assessments. *Educational Measurement: Issues and Practice, 28*(3), 5–13.

Phillips, D., Gormley, W., & Anderson, S. (2016). The effects of Tulsa's CAP head start program on middle-school academic outcomes and progress. *Developmental Psychology*, 52 (8), 1247–1261.

Phillips, O. (2015). *Revolving door of teachers costs schools billions every year.* National Public Radio ED. Retrieved January 18, 2016, from http://www.npr.org/sections/ed/2015/03/30/395322012/the-hidden-costs-of-teacher-turnover.

Pink, D. H. (2011). *Drive: The surprising truth about what motivates us.* Edinburgh: Canongate.

Poglinco, S. M., Bach, A. J., Hovde, K., Rosenblum, S., Saunders, M., & Supovitz, J. A. (2003). *The heart of the matter: The coaching model in America's Choice schools.* Philadelphia, PA: University of Pennsylvania, Consortium for Policy Research in Education.

Pollitt, E. (1991). Effects of a diet deficient in iron on the growth and development of preschool and school age children. *Food and Nutrition Bulletin*, 13(2), 110–118.

Poynor, L., & O'Malley, M. (2015). *Climate connection toolkit: Low- and no-cost activities for cultivating a supportive school climate.*

Professional development under KERA: Meeting the challenge. Lexington, KY: The Partnership for Kentucky Schools & The Prichard Committee for Academic Excellence.

Powell, S. D. (2013). Learning modalities. *PBS Parents*. Retrieved from https://www.education.com/reference/article/learning-modalities/.

Ramirez, D., & Douglas, D. (1989). *Language minority parents and the school: Can home-school partnerships increase student success?* California: California State Dept. of Education.

RAND Health. (2001). Mental health care for youth: Who gets it? How much does it cost? Who pays? Where does the money go?

Rauschenberg, S. (2014). How consistent are course grades? An examination of differential grading. *Education Policy Analysis Archives*, 22(92).

Reardon, M. (2008). Americans text more than they talk. *CNET*. September 22, 2008.

Reardon, S., & Portilla, X. (2016). Recent trends in income, racial, and ethnic school readiness gaps at kindergarten entry. *AERA Open*, 2(3), 1–18.

Reeves, D. B. (2011). *Elements of grading: A guide to effective practice.* Bloomington, IN: Solution Tree Press.

Reiff, J. C. (1992). *Learning styles.* Washington, DC: National Education Association.

Reitzug, U. C. (2002). *Professional development. School reform Proposals: The Research Evidence.*

Renzulli, J., & Smith, L. (1978). *Learning styles inventory: A measure of student preference for instructional techniques.* Mansfield Center, CT: Creative Learning Press, Inc.

Reynolds, A. (1992). What is a competent beginning teacher? A review of the literature. *Review of Educational Research*, 62, 1–35.

Roscoe, R. D., & Chi, M. T. H. (2007). Understanding tutor learning: Knowledge-building and knowledge-telling in peer tutors' explanations and questions. *Review of Educational Research*, 77(4), 534–574.

Rosenshine, B. (1986). Synthesis of research on explicit teaching. *Educational Leadership*, 43(7), 60–69.

Rosenshine, B., & Stevens, R. (1986). Teaching Functions. In M. C. Wittrock (Ed.), *Handbook of research on teaching* (3rd ed.).

Rosenthal, R., & Jacobson, L. (1968). *Pygmalion in the classroom*. New York: Holt, Rinehart & Winston.

Rossmiller, R. A. (1983). Time-on-task: A look at what erodes time for instruction. *NASSP Bulletin*, 67, 45–49.

Rovee-Collier, C. (1995). Time windows in cognitive development. *Developmental Psychology*, 31, 147–169.

Rowe, M. B. (1974). Wait-time and rewards as instructional variables, their influence on language, logic and fate control: Parts I and II. *Journal of Research in Science Teaching*, 11, 81–84, 291–308.

Ruhl, K. L., Hughes, C., & Schloss, P. (1987). Using the pause procedure to enhance lecture recall. *Teacher Education and Special Education*, 10, 14–18.

Rumberger, R. W., & Larson, K. A. (1998). Student mobility and the increased risk of high school dropout. *American Journal of Education*, 107(1), 1–35.

Rye, J. (1982). *The cloze procedure and the teaching of reading*. Oxford: Heinemann Educational Books Ltd.

Saddler, B., & Asaro-Saddler, K. (2010). Writing better sentences: Sentence-combining instruction in the classroom. *Preventing School Failure*, 54(3), 159–163.

Sanders, W., & Rivers, J. (1996). *Cumulative and residual effects of teachers on future student academic achievement*. Research Progress Report.

Schneider, E. (2000). *Summer Tutoring - Good Idea or Bad?* Available online http://www.lessontutor.com/ees11.html

Schurr, S. L. (1992). Fine tuning your parent power: Increasing student achievement. *Schools in the Middle*, 2(2), 3–9.

Sergiovanni, T. (2001). *The principalship: A reflective practice* (5th ed.). San Antonio, TX: Trinity Press.

Shoemaker, B. (1989). Integrative education. A curriculum for the twenty-first century. *OSSC Bulletin Series*. Eugene, Oregon: Oregon School Study Council.

Shouse, R. D. (1996). Academic press and sense of community: Conflict, congruence, and implications for student achievement. *Social Psychology of Education*, 1, 47–68.

Skaalvik, E., & Skaalvik, S. (2007). Dimensions of teacher self-efficacy and relationship with strain factors, perceived collective teacher efficacy, and teacher burnout. *Journal of Educational Psychology*, 99(3), 611–625.

Skinner, E., & Belmont, M. (1991). *A longitudinal study of motivation in school: Reciprocal effects of teacher behavior and student engagement*. Unpublished manuscript, University of Rochester, Rochester, NY.

Smaldino, S., Lowther, D., & Russell, J. (2007). *Instructional media and technologies for learning* (9th ed.). Englewood Cliffs: Prentice Hall, Inc.

Small, M. (2010). Beyond one right answer. *Educational Leadership*, 68(1), 28–32.

Smith, F. (2009). *Effective types of active engagement*. Paper presented at the Active Engagement and Effective Teaching Practices – A Bridge from Teaching to Learning Conference, Phoenix, AZ, February 29, 2009.

———. (2009). *Tips to better lectures, lesson plan notes, and practice*. Paper presented at the Active Engagement and Effective Teaching Practices – A Bridge from Teaching to Learning Conference, Phoenix, AZ, February 29, 2009.

Sparks, D. (2002). *Designing powerful professional development for teachers and principals.* Oxford, OH: National Staff Development Council.
Sparks, D., & Loucks-Horsley, S. (1989). Five models of staff development for teachers. *Journal of Staff Development,* 10(4), 40–57.
Sparks, S. (2016). Partnership explores role of student mental health in classroom management. *Education Week.*
Sprick, R., Garrison, M., & Howard, L. (1998). *CHAMPS: A proactive and positive approach to classroom management.* Longmont, CA: Sopris West.
Squire, J. R. (1983). Composing and comprehending: Two sides of the same basic process. *Language Arts,* 60, 581–589.
Sriarunrasmee, J., Praweenya, S., & Dachakupt, P. (2015). Virtual field trips with inquiry learning and critical thinking process: A learning model to enhance students' science learning outcome. *Procedia-Social and Behavioral Sciences,* 1721–1726.
Stahl, R. J. (1994). Using "Think-Time" and "Wait-Time" skillfully in the classroom. *ERIC Digest.* http://files.eric.ed.gov/fulltext/ED370885.pdf.
Stanovich, K. E., Cunningham, A. E., & Freeman, D. J. (1984). Intelligence, cognitive skills and early reading progress. *Reading Research Quarterly,* 19, 278–303.
Stiggins, R. J. (2008). *Assessment manifesto: A call for the development of balanced assessment systems.* Portland, OR: ETS Assessment Training Institute.
Stover, D. (2000). Schools grapple with high student mobility rates. *School Board News,* 11, 1–8.
Strangman, N., & Hall, T. (2004). *Background knowledge.* Wakefield, MA: National Center on Accessing the General Curriculum.
Stronck, D. R. (1980). The educational implications of human individuality. *American Biology Teacher,* 42, 146–151.
Strong, R., Silver, H. F., & Robinson, A. (1995). What do students want? *Educational Leadership,* 53(1), 8–12.
Strong, W. (1986). *Creative approaches to sentence combining.* Urbana, IL: ERIC Clearinghouse on Reading and Communication Skills & National Council of Teachers of English.
Stronge, J., & Hindman, J. (2003). Hiring the best teachers. *Educational Leadership,* 60(8), 48–52.
Swengel, E. M. (1991). Peer tutoring: Back to the roots of peer helping. *The Peer Facilitator Quarterly,* 8(4), 28–32.
Sykes, G. (1996). Reform of and as professional development. *Phi Delta Kappan,* 77(7).
Tauber, R. T. (1998). *Good or bad, what teachers expect from students they generally get!* ERIC document ED 426 985.
Tileston, D. (2004). *What every teacher should know about learning, memory, and the brain.* Thousand Oaks, CA: Corwin Press.
Toll, C. (2005). *The literacy coach's survival guide: Essential questions and practical answers.* International Reading Association: Newark, DE.
Tomlinson, C. A. (1999). *The differentiated classroom: Responding to the needs of all learners.* Alexandria, VA: Association for Supervision and Curriculum Development.
———. (2000). Differentiated instruction: Can it work? *The Education Digest,* 65(5), 25–31.

———. (2003). *Fulfilling the promise of the differentiated classroom: Strategies and tools for responsive teaching.* Alexandria, VA: Association for Supervision and Curriculum Development.

Tomlinson, C. A., & Allan, S. D. (2000). *Leadership for differentiating schools and classrooms.* Alexandria, VA: Association for Supervision and Curriculum Development.

Tomlinson, C. A. & Eidson, C. C. (2003). Differentiation in practice: A resource guide for differentiating curriculum. Alexandria, VA: Association for Supervision and Curriculum Development.

Tomlinson, C. A. & McTighe, J. (2006). *Integrating differentiated instruction and understanding by design.* Alexandria, VA: Association for Supervision and Curriculum Development.

Topping, K. (1996). The effectiveness of peer tutoring in further and education: A typology and review of the literature. *Higher Education,* 32, 321–345.

Tsui, A. (1995). *Introducing Classroom Interaction.* London: Penguin.

Tyler, R. W. (1950). *Basic principles of curriculum and instruction.* Chicago: University of Chicago Press.

Udelhofen, S. (2005). *Keys to curriculum mapping: strategies and tools to make it work.* Thousand Oaks, CA: Corwin Press.

U.S. Bureau of Justice Statistics (2004). *Survey of Inmates in State and Federal Correctional Facilities.* Washington, DC: U.S. Department of Justice.

Verdugo, R., & Schneider, J. (1999). Quality schools, safe schools: A theoretical and empirical discussion. *Education & Urban Society,* 31(3), 286–308.

Voke, H. (2002). Motivating students to learn. *ASCD Infobrief,* 2(28).

Vygotsky, L. (1962). *Thought and language.* Cambridge, MA: The MIT Press.

———. (1978). *Mind in society: The development of higher psychological processes.* Cambridge, MA: Harvard University Press.

Walker, D. (2004). *What every teacher should know about student motivation.* Corwin Pr.

Walker, G., Audette, R., & Algozzine, R. (1998). Increasing time on task through total quality education. *ERS Spectrum,* 16(3), 11–16.

Wherry, H. (1996). 1996 NAESP Convention, Washington, DC, March 24,1996.

Wenglinsky, H. (2000). *How teaching matters: Bringing the classroom back into discussions of teacher quality.* Princeton, NJ: Educational Testing Service.

WestEd: West Comprehensive Center (2015). *Workbook for improving school climate and closing the achievement gap.* Retrieved from https://www.wested.org/online_pubs/WB_1221_allv5.pdf.

WestEd: West Comprehensive Center (2015). *California School Climate Survey (CSCS).* Retrieved from https://www.wested.org/project/california-school-climate-survey-cscs/.

Westbrook, F. (2011). Lessons from the other side of the teacher's desk: Discovering insights to help language learners. *English Teaching Forum,* 49(1), 2–7.

Wiggins, G. (1998). *Educative assessment: Designing assessments to inform and improve student performance.* San Francisco: Jossey-Bass.

Williams, W. M., Blythe, T., White, N., Li, J., Sternberg, R. J., & Gardner, H. (1996). *Practical intelligence for school.* New York: HarperCollins College Publishers.

Wong, H., & Wong, R. (1991). *The first days of school: How to be an effective teacher*. California: Harry Wong Publications.

Woods, E. G. (1995). Reducing the dropout rate. In *School improvement research series (SIRS): Research you can use (Close-up No. 17)*. Portland, OR: Northwest Regional Educational Laboratory.

Wrześniewski, A., Schwartz, B., Cong, X., Kane, M., Omar, A., & Kolditz, T. (2014). Multiple types of motives don't multiply the motivation of West Point cadets. *Proceedings of the National Academy of Sciences*, 111(30).

Yazzie-Mintz, E. (2007). *Voices of students on engagement: A report on the 2006 High School Survey of Student Engagement*. Bloomington, IN: Center for Evaluation & Education Policy, Indiana University.

Yelland, N., & Masters, J. (2007). Rethinking scaffolding in the information age. *Computers and Education*, 48, 362–382.

Younger, D. S. (2017). Epidemiology of childhood mental illness: A review of U.S. surveillance data and the literature. *World Journal of Neuroscience*, 7, 48–54.

About the Authors

Shelly Pollnow received her EdD in Policy and Administration from Arizona State University, her MEd in Curriculum and Instruction and Elementary Education from Arizona State University, and her BS in Business Administration from Grand Canyon University. She has spent over 20 years of her education career in Arizona teaching diverse learners in Grades 1 through 6 as an inclusion classroom teacher as well as a gifted program teacher. Dr. Pollnow has also been involved in professional development for teachers and has nationally presented her research on implementing professional development in formative assessment at the classroom level. She has been the Arizona Director of the National Assessment of Educational Progress and international assessment programs since 2011 and has served on the Formative Assessment for Students and Teachers CCSSO SCASS since 2012.

Oran Tkatchov's educational career has included such roles as a middle school teacher, high school teacher, and charter school director. He has an additional 11 years of experience directing, presenting, and providing professional development in the areas of special education, leadership, and school/district improvement at the Arizona Department of Education. He currently supports professional learning initiatives for the Arizona State Schools for the Deaf and the Blind. He received his MEd in Educational Leadership from Northern Arizona University and is a Level 1 Google Certified Educator and a certified facilitator for the National Institute for School Leadership.

CONTACT INFORMATION

Shelly Pollnow

Email: shellypollnow@gmail.com
Twitter: @skpollnow
www.successforeverystudent.com
www.trueperformancelearning.com

Oran Tkatchov

Email: orantkatchov@gmail.com
Twitter: @orantkatchov
www.successforeverystudent.com
www.trueperformancelearning.com

www.ingramcontent.com/pod-product-compliance
Lightning Source LLC
Chambersburg PA
CBHW021851300426
44115CB00005B/106